FIVE STONES AND A SLING

To Clare, my companion through the life of which this is the narrative, my support in good times and bad, who took down the text at my dictation, and materially improved it with her comments.

FIVE STONES AND A SLING

MEMOIRS OF A BIBLICAL SCHOLAR

Michael Goulder

SHEFFIELD PHOENIX PRESS

2009

Copyright © 2009 Sheffield Phoenix Press

Published by Sheffield Phoenix Press
Department of Biblical Studies, University of Sheffield
Sheffield S3 7QB

www.sheffieldphoenix.com

A CIP catalogue record for this book
is available from the British Library

Typeset by ISB Typesetting
Printed on acid-free paper by Lightning Source UK Ltd, Milton Keynes

ISBN 978-1-906055-84-4

CONTENTS

Chapter 1

EDUCATION

My father, Douglas Goulder (to rhyme with shoulder or boulder), was a broker on Lloyd's; that is, he arranged insurance for ships and their cargoes both British and European at competitive rates with Lloyd's underwriters in the City of London. A large man—he was 6 ft 4 and sixteen stone—he was friendly and active, a popular and respected figure in all aspects of his life; when he was killed in the War my mother received something like 230 letters of condolence, from people in many walks of life and half a dozen countries in Europe, all testifying to his kindness and friendship. He had married my mother Daphne, a kind and intelligent woman, in 1925, and I was born in May 1927 in South Kensington, a suitably middle-class area of London. My parents were not churchgoers, so apart from my baptism I had little introduction to religion in early days; I was escorted, unwillingly and irregularly, to Sunday afternoon service in St Jude's, Courtfield Gardens, by the Stapletons, a pious family with a pretty daughter, Mary, who lived across the square from us. But it was at Wagner's, a pre-prep school, the best, it was believed, in London, that I joined the Church of England from the heart. There Mr Lefroy, scarlet with emotion, told us the terrible tale of the Marian burnings, and of Latimer's brave words, 'Be of good cheer, Master Ridley; we shall this day light such a candle as I trust shall never be put out'. No, I thought, and while I live, that candle shall not go out. Wagner's told my father that I was clever, and this suggested to him a great series of hurdles which I should leap in life—public school, Cambridge, and 'the diplomatic'. With this progress in view, he made plain to me his high expectations. In the many letters he later wrote to me, he never ceased exhorting me to shine in all departments of life. His advice was the same that Peleus gave to his son Achilles, 'Always to come first and to excel others' (*aien aristeuein kai hypeirochon emmenai allon*). I should come top in both languages and maths, and be in the teams for cricket and football, and learn to ride, and to box. Where my gifts were lacking he felt he could supplement them by arranging coaching for me. Although these expectations sometimes felt oppressive, I have no doubt that his constant support and encouragement set me on the right path in life and inspired me to hard work and to success.

At the age of eight I left Wagner's and was sent to Highfield, a boarding school eighty miles away in Hampshire. Canon Mills, the Headmaster-owner, known to the boys as 'Bug', had built the school up since the beginning of the century, and established it as a respected 'feeder' to the public schools; he had retained the services of an excellent staff of assistant masters. Perhaps he was a little too fond of the slipper and the hairbrush, but he was by no means the sadistic tyrant that we liked to paint him. In his own view he was a kind old man, never happier than when reading *Nicholas Nickleby* or *All Quiet on the Western Front* to a roomful of boys in his study; and I remember such readings with pleasure. He always did his best for me, and quickly sensed that I might gain an Eton scholarship, an idea totally acceptable to my father. I was, however, not happy at the school, and some blame for this must rest with Bug himself. Wagner's had told him that I was clever, and had mastered the elements of Latin and French, so I was entered into the fifth form from the top of the school, in which the boys were mostly aged eleven. Week by week each form was stood up in line and its marks read out to the school; and week by week I went up to the top of the class. Bug's solution to this was to give me a double remove in my second term; so I was in the third form from the top of the school, in a class of mostly rather slow boys aged thirteen. It was not until my final year that my coevals caught up with me in the top form. This meant that I had to contend with loneliness, because there were never boys in my class with whom I could become friends; and also with a certain resentment, for naturally my classmates did not take kindly to being outshone by a boy three years younger than them. Bug had built a fine chapel in the middle of the school, and he was serious about our religion, preparing us for Confirmation. But his religion was on the dry side: he gave each of us a copy of *The Holy Communion* by W. Walsham How. The service was printed on the left-hand page, and on the right some edifying comments—'You are coming to God. God is coming to you. This is not a thought lightly to be dismissed.' As a biddable lad, I did not dismiss it lightly, but I found the weekly practice of meeting these words somewhat daunting. I did not greatly value Bug at the time; but I remember him now for two things in the Chapel. One was his practice of reading Ecclesiastes 12 on the last morning of each term, 'Remember now thy Creator in the days of thy youth...' The other was the moving tune which he composed to the hymn 'Souls of men, why will ye scatter?'

Bug prepared me well for the Eton Scholarship, and I sat the exam in May 1940, while the Army was being evacuated from Dunkirk. When the results came out I had won the Second Scholarship, and in the September began five delightful years at a school which might well justify its claim to be the best in the country. There were many good teachers, foremost among whom for me was Richard Martineau, whose kindliness and intense love of the Greek and Latin classics made his teaching a blessing to all his pupils. But above all I made friends for the first time, some of them friends for life; I was a mild social success, and even rose to the high point of being elected to 'Pop', the Eton Society, to whom much of the school discipline was deputed. The only shadow on my Eton years was my succumbing to polio in August 1941; this involved three months away from school, in the Wingfield Hospital at Oxford; and a difficult January term, when I came back to school half-time, and was not kindly treated by some of my fellow-Scholars.

Eton education was based on two foundations, which stood in some tension. One of these was Christianity. The School had been founded, exactly five hundred years before I was admitted, as the College of the Blessed Virgin Mary. Each morning at 9.25 the school assembled in College Chapel; there, between the soaring Perpendicular pillars raised in the Wars of the Roses, to repeat, in creed, hymn and psalm the articles of Christian belief. Every evening at 9.30 the scholars would assemble in Lower School for evening prayers, on Sundays said and sung in Latin. Between these two times the main staple was the Greek and Latin classics. The authors who had the greatest impact on us were Plato and Homer. Plato thought that one should be wary of accepted wisdom, and sceptical of anything proclaimed with confidence and authority. Richard Martineau was an enthusiastic disciple of Plato and of his teacher Socrates; we were constantly urged to think for ourselves and to challenge all dogmas, which in fact included Christian dogmas. Above all, the search for truth had primacy. Socrates represented himself as like a midwife, delivering the truth which was latent in even simple people; one had only to ask questions, and to follow wherever the answers led. Homer thought that life was a tragedy. On the whole the gods were against us, and were too strong for us. We could not win in the battle of life, but we could live nobly. Although the Gospel also urges us to live nobly, it has a happy ending in the Resurrection, which is lacking in the Iliad.

Eton prepared me well for the Scholarship examination to Cambridge, and I won a Major Scholarship to Trinity, the most prestigious of the Cambridge colleges. But I owed the award in part to my native wit. I had to translate an English poem into Greek verses in the metre used by

Sophocles. My problem was with the phrase, 'charmed by the god', which had to go into the second half of an iambic line; but I did not know the Greek for 'charm', so I cast about, and it occurred to me that 'mesmerize' was similar in meaning, and it sounded like a Greek derivation, in the same way that 'baptize' was derived from the Greek 'baptizo'. I did not know if there was such a Greek verb, but if there was 'mesmeristhentes theo' would fit the line exactly; and so I put it in. I was in fact unlucky: the word derives from Mesmer, a Swiss hypnotist of the nineteenth century! Nevertheless, I got credit for my ingenuity.

I went up to Trinity in January 1946. Cambridge was full of ex-servicemen, many of whom were not much interested in an eighteen-year-old schoolboy. My two closest Eton friends had gone to Oxford, and I found myself lonely and unhappy. After a fortnight I was visited by a stranger, David Watson. He had been to Eton, and was calling to be friendly. He asked me if I would like to go with him to the CICCU sermon next Sunday. CICCU stands for the Cambridge Inter-Collegiate Christian Union (pronounced Kick-you), and I had been warned against it. I was however so lonely that I would have been prepared to go to a bullfight or a nude show had it been suggested. So I went to the sermon, and it was indeed a shock. It was the first time that I had encountered Christianity as a religion of salvation, very different from the pallid gospel of Highfield and Eton. CICCU speakers spoke seriously: they could persuade their audience that they were in peril of eternal death, and that salvation was possible only by conversion. It soon became evident to me that David was a serious Christian such as I had not met before. He rose at six each morning and prayed and read the Bible for more than an hour. Since people like me were in eternal peril, he felt it his duty to bring the gospel to them; and if I were serious, I must do the same.

Being a member of CICCU brought its tensions, as I was soon to discover. The first of these arose from its belief in the inerrancy of Scripture. David encouraged me to give up a week of my Easter vacation to attend a conference at Oxford. I had a room in Lincoln College, and before lunch a group of eight or so was standing round the fire, talking. Someone made a remark implying that Adam and Eve were the first human beings, and in my surprise I asked him, 'Don't you believe in evolution?' The words were out of my mouth before I realized their total heresy, but instead of replying, as he could, 'Don't you believe in the truth of the Bible?' he looked embarrassed and said nothing. Fortified by this success, I went round the group, asking each of them the same question. They were all embarrassed, but were saved by the bell for lunch. A friendly man came and sat next to me, and after the meal took me for a walk; as we went along he produced a Bible from his pocket and began to explain that Darwin really agreed with Genesis. He knew more than I did, but I could smell intellectual dishonesty a yard off, and was having none of it. The pressure to evangelize was also a difficulty. The final speaker was an expert at his craft. He told us of a Christian who was travelling by train, and the Lord said to him, 'Why don't you ask the man opposite if he has been saved?' The Christian was a coward and did not dare do so. But a little later the Lord brought up the question again, and this time he responded. The man was converted, and became a missionary in Africa, and saved the souls of thousands. Now, unsurprisingly, I was going home by train, and the Lord made this same suggestion to me: but the person opposite me was a rosy-cheeked woman nursing a basket of purchases. I thought, reasonably, that any such approach would cause embarrassment and do no good, so I held my peace. However the journey from Oxford to Egham, my home station, was in two parts: GWR to Reading, and then SR for the rest. For this second leg I found myself in a compartment with what seemed to be a businessman looking over the company accounts. I thought, slightly dishonestly, that I might expect a sign from heaven before speaking: if the man were still there after the next station, and nobody joined us, I would speak. We passed the station, and he and I were still alone in the compartment; I reached up into my bag for a copy of Scripture, hoping to light on a less crude formula than, 'Have you been saved?' The man looked up: 'Do you belong to the Christian Union?' he asked. 'Marvellous, isn't it? I have been a member for twenty-five years'. I felt like Abraham seeing the ram in the thicket.

I am now surprised at my simplicity; but group pressure is a powerful force. CICCU speakers were commonly men of deep conviction. A significant figure in my time was Basil Atkinson, a man whose devotion was so strong as to raise questions about his balance of mind. Speaking of heaven at a public service in the Marketplace at Cambridge, he was heckled: 'What do you know about heaven?' 'My dear fellow', came the answer, vibrant with emotion, 'I live there'. During a Bible-reading at Trinity he said, 'Russia has never been evangelized. I am trying to make arrangements to be parachuted in with some Russian Bibles. If any of you speak Russian, you may feel called to join me'. Fortunately the RAF did not take kindly to the idea of risking a bomber to parachute a group of loonies into Russia; so I was spared what would surely have been a short step to a Siberian grave.

The crisis came in August. David had urged me to give a week of my summer vacation to be an 'officer' at a so-called Harvest Camp in

Somerset. During the War there had been a shortage of labour to bring in the harvest, and public schoolboys had been urged to go down to farms and work. A clergyman called Nash had seen this as an opportunity: the harvest of crops could be combined with a harvest of souls. Each year, and on into peacetime too, he would organize accommodation for a week, especially for boys whose parents were for some reason abroad. This would then give him opportunity to evangelize the teenagers after their day's work in the fields. But by 1946 no actual fieldwork was undertaken. The week was a holiday camp with well-organized games and concerts, and also of Bible-readings and prayers. The first two evenings the prayers were reassuringly low-key, with a short talk by one of the officers. The third evening was taken by Nash himself, and was full-pelt evangelism: he showed a large print of Holman Hunt's 'The Light of the World', and preached to the text, 'Behold I stand at the door and knock'. It was an experienced and skilled evangelist against virtually defenceless fifteen-year-olds. They stood no chance of independent judgement, and I felt ashamed to be associated with such proceedings. I understood only too well how vulnerable they were. But this was not the only problem. I was not prepared to be intellectually dishonest over biblical inerrancy. Genesis 1 was contradicted by the theory of evolution, and was also inconsistent with Genesis 2. After the harvest camp I resigned my unsought position as College Rep, and left the CICCU. I then joined the more normal, sane, but ineffective body, the Student Christian Movement.

Chapter 2

Jardine Matheson's

By 1948 I had spent three years at Cambridge, preparing myself for life: now the last examination was finally written, and it was time to move on; but I had no idea what I should do next. The University had an Appointments Board, a kind of upmarket jobcentre, and it was thither that I went for some advice. Mr Singer was friendly and helpful. Had I any money? No? Then I was too late to train for a profession. My choice effectively was between business and the Civil Service. As I had no obvious business contact, he recommended the Civil Service. Entry was normally by examination, and as I was good at exams I should be able to get in. As so often, professional advice is wise but may be mistaken. The letter came advising me of the date and place of the examination; and to my dismay the date was the same as that on which I had agreed with three friends to go for a month's holiday to Italy. The rail tickets had been bought and the couchettes booked, as well as beds in various *pensioni* around Italy. It took only a moment's hesitation to prefer my holiday to my chance of becoming Sir Humphrey Appleby. I was right. We had a marvellous time, and my abilities would have been wasted in the Civil Service. So it was back to Mr Singer. It had to be business then: did I want to work in Britain or abroad? Abroad sounded more venturesome, and there was a post advertised with a firm, Jardine, Matheson, and Co., a long-established trading company with interests all over China.

I went up for the interview at its London office, Matheson and Co., 3 Lombard St, London, E.C. The address was redolent of commercial power and stability. The office overlooked the Bank of England on one side, and the church of St Mary Woolnoth on the other. The atmosphere here was less impressive: T.S. Eliot writes of the Unreal City where the crowd of clerks streams 'across the bridge and down King William Street, To where St Mary Woolnoth tolls the hours, With a dead sound on the final stroke of nine'. The firm was pleased to engage me, and I was told by an Old China Hand of the perils and privations of life in that great country; when he had been there, there was no lavatory paper.

I was three months working for Matheson's, learning the London end of the business. This was largely concerned with financing shipments from London to Shanghai or Hong Kong. One of our most frequent clients was the French firm Peugeot, which would despatch consignments of scissors to China. A cheerful clerk would proudly announce, 'Another order from Peugeot', but as his education had not included the French language, this was always pronounced 'Pugo', to rhyme with Hugo. As a Scottish firm, Matheson's took a pride in never giving things away. The firm imported jars of ginger in syrup from China, and in November an offer was made to the staff to buy these at five shillings a jar; I noticed identical jars soon afterwards on sale at the same price in the shops. My mother was fond of ginger so I bought a jar; but I did not wish to take it home at once where she would see it. The jars had reliable-looking screw-tops, so I thought I would stand my jar upright in a drawer of the desk where I was seated. Unfortunately the drawer was not deep enough to permit the jar to be stood upright, so I laid it on its side, on top of a pile of the firm's old correspondence. When Christmas time came I returned to the drawer with a bag in which to take my jar home. To my dismay the screw-top had not been reliable, and about an inch of the syrup had ebbed out, causing the firm's correspondence to be rather less legible. I might have confessed my error to the office manager, but I felt that the sale had not been very generous, and by the time the syrup was discovered, I should be safely beyond the Suez Canal.

So, on 9 January 1949, I set sail in the cargo liner *Glengarry* for Hong Kong. The journey took three and a half weeks, and the Glen Line had provided for the entertainment of the eighteen passengers a radiogram and six records, one of them 'A Slow Boat to China'.

It became clear to me soon after arrival in the colony that the job with Jardine's was a mistake. This was partly the fault of those who had interviewed me. The firm was owned by a group of Lowland Scottish families, who sent their sons to the East to run the firm: so the Directors were all called Landale, or Keswick or such names, and there was no place in the Private Office for anyone to be promoted on grounds of ability. My prospects were thus extremely limited. I was also unlucky. Jardine's had developed in the course of a century an enormous commercial empire covering much of China: it owned docks, wharves, go-downs (warehouses), breweries, cotton mills, an airline, and so on. My dreams of sharing in the direction of this great enterprise had in fact been shattered the previous month. In December, 1948, Mao Tse-Tung's Communist armies defeated the Nationalist armies of Chiang Kai-Shek. As the new Government took over more and more of China they closed foreign-owned businesses and expelled their Western staff.

Worse still, life at Jardine's was corrupting. I was put in the Secretary's Office, where the work was to buy and sell shares for the firm and for its directors. It did not take me long to learn how to evaluate a company report and to analyse a balance sheet, so I soon began to buy and sell on my own account. Success was intoxicating. I was able to secure a loan from the Hongkong Bank, and persuaded some of my colleagues to entrust their savings to me, forming a syndicate called 'Goulder Unlimited'. Thus the way opened towards a wasted life of speculation and gambling, a long way from the high ideals with which I had begun. Moreover, there was a temptation of a different kind. I shared an office with an extremely attractive young married woman, Tamara. I should have known better than to be tempted, and neither my loneliness nor our enforced propinquity was any excuse. I am grateful to `Mara for not enticing me to serious fault, which she might well have done. For she was no saint, and soon afterwards met a titled Army officer, and deserted her husband to become a countess. Nor was the atmosphere in the Mess any more improving than that in the office. My colleagues spent their leisure at the races or in yachts. The firm paid for the juniors to have lessons in Cantonese if they were willing to come to the office an hour early; but I was the only member of the Mess to take advantage of this. My Cantonese became useful, though never fluent; Chinese is a difficult language, and it would need a two-year course to achieve real fluency.

Chapter 3

St John's Cathedral

In this Wasteland my recourse was to the Cathedral, a century-old Gothic building, half an hour's walk down the hill from the Mess. Alaric Rose, the Dean, was an interesting preacher, and a good pastor. He greeted me after the service and invited me to dinner. After this I was often invited to Sunday dinner at the Roses'. There were usually around twenty guests, drawn from all walks of Hong Kong life—including some Chinese!—and the conversation was far more interesting and instructive than that in the Mess. Furthermore there was a constant stream of missionaries who had been expelled from China by the new Government, and who had come to Hong Kong on their way through to England or America. It was very interesting to hear their impressions of life in the new China.

Alaric introduced me to the Bishop, R.O. Hall, widely known by his initials as 'R.O.' The first thing that struck me about him was the simplicity of his living. He wore a plain purple shirt, with no rings or pectoral cross or other episcopal flummery. The meal with which he entertained me was a plain Chinese bowl of soup and one of rice. The Bishop's house was a plain colonial house, of which half was given over for the Dean to live in, and the main room in the Bishop's half had been turned into a chapel; the upstairs had been divided into flats and living quarters for various church workers who could not find affordable accommodation. R.O. had given most of the garden area to provide the site for a hospital. He had bought a small piece of land on a hill above Sha Tin in the New Territories, and built a Chinese-style house on it, with a simple chapel. R.O. used to work late into the evening in the house in Hong Kong, and it was often midnight before he and Mrs Hall would start their hour's journey by car across the harbour and out to their rural retreat. Mrs Hall made a beautiful garden there, full of bougainvillea and roses, and R.O. had added a flat above the garage for the holiday use of the clergy and other guests. The whole place had an atmosphere of beauty and peace.

R.O. was an imaginative and courageous bishop, who has left his mark on the history of the Church. In 1943 the Japanese were occupying South

China, with occasional massacres, and those who could fled across the border into Macao, which as a Portuguese colony was neutral territory. This presented R.O. with a problem: the vicar of Macao was a peasant-priest, and not suited to be the pastor of the often well-educated refugees. But the only cleric with a degree who was available was a deaconess, Lei Tim Oi. A deaconess would be unable to celebrate Holy Communion, so if she were appointed the congregation would have no sacrament, and if she were not appointed they would have no competent teaching. R.O. consulted his suffragan, Bishop Mok, who came up with a ready suggestion: why not ordain Lei Tim Oi a priest? The idea had obvious attractions, but R.O. knew it would arouse strong opposition, and the Anglican Church as a whole might refuse to ratify his action. St Paul had said that women should keep silent in church, and be subject to men; and there was an unbroken tradition over two millennia in the Catholic, Anglican and Orthodox Churches that only men could be priests. The resistance would be rooted in deep non-theological factors, the prejudice that women are inferior, the contempt felt for South China as the back of beyond, and the fear of disapproval in Rome. So R.O. wrote to two influential friends, William Temple, Archbishop of York, and Reinhold Niebuhr, a respected American theologian. I do not know how Temple responded, but Niebuhr wrote back encouragingly: it would be a major step forward, to be compared with the admission of Gentiles into the Church in St Peter's time, when Cornelius was baptized without circumcision. So, in 1944, in a small village up-country from Canton, Lei Tim Oi was priested by R.O., the first woman to be so. It was the custom for Chinese [male] to be given Western names on their ordination, and when R.O. wrote to Niebuhr to describe the occasion he said, 'I resisted the temptation to give her the name Cornelia'. R.O. knew he would face opposition, but he did not know the humiliations to which he would be exposed. The rumour of what he had done was soon current, and when the Navy came to liberate Hong Kong, chaplains went through his papers in search of incriminating documents. The Anglican Church held a Lambeth Conference of all its bishops in 1948. By then Temple had died, and had been succeeded by Geoffrey Fisher as Archbishop of Canterbury. R.O. persuaded the other Chinese bishops to put a motion to the Conference that for twenty years the Chung Hua Shing Hui (the Chinese Province of the Anglican Church) should be permitted to have ordained women; but thanks to Fisher's opposition the motion was lost, and the other Chinese bishops later withdrew their support for what R.O. had done.

Thus R.O. lost the first round; but he won in the end. He retired from his diocese in 1963, and was succeeded by the kindly and well-meaning

Gilbert Baker, described by Bishop Wilson of Birmingham as 'a muddler of muddlers'. But Gilbert surprised the doubters: he rallied the bishops of South East Asia to support his ordaining two further women priests, Jane Hwang, who became the successful Vicar of St Thomas', Shekkipmei, and Joyce Bennett, who proved to be an effective speaker for the [English] Movement for the Ordination of Women. In 1992 the Synod of the Church of England voted to ordain women priests; and 'e'en the ranks of Tuscany could scarce forbear to cheer'. A short time later Carlo Martini, Cardinal Archbishop of Milan, was asked if the [Catholic] Church would ever ordain women; he replied sagely, 'Not in this millennium'.

Before he went to China, R.O. had been vicar of a poor parish, St Luke's, Newcastle, during the slump of the early 1930s; and so became very conscious of the problems of poverty. This made him sympathetic to the reforms introduced by the new Communist Government in his diocese in South China. I asked him whether the Chinese were confiscating Church property, and he said, 'The Catholic Church is one of the largest landowners in China. The Government's policy is land reform, so that the land may belong to those who work it. They thus have the motivation to get the most out of it, and they receive the reward for their labour'. This approbation of Communist policies caused R.O. to have the reputation of being 'red', but he was merely conscious that the old landlord system had been exploitative of the farm-workers.

Similarly he devoted much energy to social problems in Hong Kong. Chinese people believed that education was the ladder by which their children could climb out of poverty; and R.O. sponsored a policy of enormous investment in Church schools. He built primary and secondary schools, Chinese-language and English-language schools, boys' schools and girls' schools. I commented to him that girls in Catholic schools looked much smarter than those in Anglican ones, with their white uniforms and green sashes; he said, 'We decided that the uniform in all Anglican girls' schools should be plain blue; and the mothers bless us every day for saving them the washing'. In 1950 there was a considerable influx of learned refugees into the colony; and he saw this as an opportunity for founding a second, Chinese-speaking, University. Hong Kong University had some good scholars, but also some lazy, seedy and even drink-sodden expatriate staff; but since the language of instruction was English, the door was virtually shut to those whose secondary education had been in Chinese. A new university was a huge project, requiring land and much money: it was R.O. who had the vision to press for it, and it was built in a few years in the New Territories. R.O. tried to give a lead to the Government in many areas: he started a

Housing Association, a Family Welfare Service, a Discharged Prisoners Aid Society, and other similar ventures. Often, in time, the Government was shamed into expanding these initiatives. The Governor was advised by a Council of millionaire businessmen and civil servants, and so it is no wonder that income tax was set at only 10%.

I asked R.O. if there was anything I could do to help with any of his projects, and he suggested that I might like to go and visit one of the clubs run by the Boys' and Girls' Clubs Association, which were held in Church premises for children not attending school. So I began to go one evening a week to a club at St Matthew's, Shaukiwan. As my Chinese was still very inadequate, there was not much I could do, but I joined in the games. A friend had taught me a Chinese version of 'Who's afraid of the Big Bad Wolf?'—'*Been-goh pa ni-go dai lo-foo*'. Actually *lo-foo* means a tiger, and I was accorded the nickname *dai lo-foo* by the boys. When it was Christmas-time I gave the club leader a hundred dollars (about £8), and this was enough to buy a jersey for each boy in the club.

About this time Alaric made me a proposal. I was obviously unhappy with Jardine's, and my heart was in the Church. Would I consider seeking ordination? I could work on the Cathedral staff, first as a Reader, then as a deacon from Advent 1950, and finally as a priest. There was no theological college in Hong Kong but this would be no obstacle. I could go to Oxford when I returned to England, and study with Austin Farrer, a much-respected scholar with whom Alaric had studied earlier. In the meantime I could have some preliminary studies with Alaric himself and with the Bishop. The practical details of being a parson I would have to learn by doing them; on the whole R.O. preferred this to the hothouse atmosphere of a theological college.

I thought carefully about this and consulted some old friends; and the idea seemed a good one. I would have to leave Jardine's Mess, but I was offered a job as Warden of a Toc H house, and I could live there. So the die was cast, and I had two years on the Cathedral staff, which on the whole passed happily. I took the Sunday School, taught a Confirmation class, visited the Cathedral congregation in their homes, and the sick in hospital. It was often a baptism by fire: Alaric might phone me with the news that one of the Sunday School children had died; would I call on the parents and arrange and take the funeral? I was extremely nervous fulfilling such duties, but at least commonsense prevented me from saying anything phoney, like 'of course God cares'.

Toc H had been founded in Ypres in 1917 to provide a house to which soldiers away from the front could come. Hong Kong in 1950 was awash with soldiers who had been sent to keep the [Chinese] People's Liberation

Army out of the Colony; and many of these would be glad of the facilities provided by such a house. The Government had in fact given such a house to Toc H, a confiscated Japanese property; but the organization had no funds with which to maintain it and solved the problem by letting the bedrooms to local residents. I had one such bedroom, but it seemed absurd for the house to be given to Toc H and not used for its purpose. As I also had a small octagonal office I moved my belongings and bed there and used the bedroom for three soldiers on leave. The residents were not best pleased to be sharing their dining-room with squaddies, but they respected the fact that I had given up my room to make space for them.

I was made a deacon in St John's Cathedral on Advent Sunday 1950, and a priest a year later on 21 December 1951. To the Church it is the latter which is the more important: only a priest has authority to celebrate Holy Communion, and the title is a universal symbol of a mediator between God and people. But to me it was becoming a deacon which was the more significant: at this service I became a clergyman. It was conducted by R.O. with the greatest dignity, and his own devoted exercise of the office was both a challenge and an inspiration. Alaric preached the sermon, on the text from Ecclesiasticus, 'The wisdom of the scribe cometh with leisure'. He spoke of the duty of a minister to take adequate time to read and to think; but as a scholar of Plato he also laid stress on the quest for truth as a primary requirement. I found the sermon surprising as my own ideals had been more practical, but in fact what he said has been a guide to much of my later life. I have been a reading and thinking minister, whose ultimate concern has not been the repetition of Church orthodoxy but rather a willingness to follow the truth wherever it took me.

I worked happily on the Cathedral staff for a further year and a half, busy with normal pastoral duties. I organized the Cathedral Fair in the autumn of 1951; I preached my first sermons, gave talks and Confirmation courses; I learned from China missionaries better ways of conducting the Sunday School; I edited the *St John's Review*, sometimes unwisely provoking controversy. After eighteen happy months, I said farewell in June 1952. I sailed for England via Bombay, where I stayed with my old friend Robin Macnaghten. He had had a somewhat parallel career to my own, working for his family's firm; but this was not his calling, and soon afterwards he also returned to England where he became a successful schoolmaster at Eton, and in time a triumphant Headmaster at Sherborne. I went on overland by train from Basra to Baghdad, by bus across the desert to Damascus, by taxi to Amman, and on to Jerusalem. These travels were not without their perils. A policeman stopped the taxi as we crossed from Syria into Jordan; the driver got out a mile later, unscrewed the door panel and revealed hundreds of sunglasses which he was smuggling in. So it was this that the policeman was looking for and I had no need to be so nervous when he went through my bags. Jerusalem presented difficulties as half the city was in Israeli hands and half in those of Jordan. I had to carry two passports in order to move from one to the other, and as I strolled along the frontier on the Arab side I was commanded to halt at gunpoint. I was taken to the police-station, and had another nervous moment trying to be sure that I produced the correct passport. I greatly enjoyed a tour of the sites of the Old City. I called at a convent which advertized that it enclosed the *Lithostrotos,* the Pavement on which Pilate judged Jesus. The door was eventually opened by a nun, a beautiful but ill-tempered woman. It emerged in conversation that she combined other duties with displaying the Pavement to visitors who were often rather casual tourists. She had taken me for one of these, so I revealed to her that I was a pious Anglican priest on a pilgrimage. She pointed to my informal dress, which I excused on the ground that I was on holiday. The sharp reply came back, 'Our priests are never on holiday'.

I continued my journey by boat from Haifa to Cyprus, and thence to Naples. I had intended to thumb a lift up Italy and across France; but soon discovered to my cost that the custom of thumbing a lift was unknown to Italian drivers, who shouted cheerily to me, 'Autobus! Autobus!' So I ended my travels by coach and train, and was happy to reach England and my home, Wingfield, at Englefield Green, without mishap. After I had been a few weeks there, my mother took me and my two brothers for a holiday to Gleneagles Hotel in the Trossachs. My next port of call was Oxford, where I was to pursue my theological studies.

Chapter 4

Oxford

I found myself satisfactory digs in Walton Road with Mrs Fagan, a delightful and motherly widow of a clergyman. She was pleased to have a young priest as lodger, though I was not High-Church enough for her taste. I had the cheapest room in the house, on the top floor, and pursued an ascetic life with cold baths each morning through the winter. I went to see Roy Lee, the Vicar of St Mary's, the University Church: R.O. was anxious that I should not lose my pastoral zeal in the sands of academic theology, and had arranged for me to be part-time curate there. This had two advantages. It provided a ready introduction to the many interesting people in St Mary's congregation; and it also provided a welcome thirty shillings a week to keep my head above water. I did not want to ask my mother for further money towards my education, and, rather quixotically, felt I should not ask the Church to subsidize me either. I had enough money saved from Hong Kong to cover my fees at Trinity College, but the small stipend from St Mary's helped with everyday living. Roy Lee was a kind man, an Australian Chinese who had made his reputation with a book called 'Freud and Christianity', and by his work as Religious Affairs Director for the BBC. The job at St Mary's was, however, I always felt, too big for him. The church was historic. Cranmer had been tried in it, before walking to the stake in Broad Street. Newman had been the Vicar in the 1830s and had launched the Oxford Movement from its pulpit. Roy's two predecessors, George Cockin and Dick Milford, had established the custom of inviting notable preachers to service on Sunday evenings. Roy lacked their charisma; he was not a great preacher nor an impressive theological thinker, but he was able to continue this tradition through my time, with a following of undergraduates sufficient to fill the large church, even the gallery, with a discussion afterwards in the Old Library. Oxford was a highly competitive place, with successful preachers at the evangelical St Aldate's, the Anglo-Catholic Pusey House, and numerous college chapels. Roy's mild Liberalism was not much with which to withstand such lively alternatives. He had another curate, John Grimwade, whom I found brash and insensitive, though he was also hardworking and sincere, and Roy had difficulty standing up to some of his unwelcome initiatives. I had two happy years working with Roy, and it was thanks to him that the flat on the top floor of the Vicarage in Holywell Street was put at my disposal. This was particularly helpful, as it turned out, for I had met a student, Clare Gardner, who was in her last year at Lady Margaret Hall, to whom I became engaged in January 1953; and so, after we had got married, she was able to join me there.

I went on to Trinity to meet Austin Farrer, who immediately impressed me with his learning and religious devotion. He was a slight figure with a scholar's face, and a friendly manner. When he had asked me a little about my background he got down to business: had I read any books about the New Testament? I replied, rather too confidently, that I had read Streeter's *The Four Gospels*. Austin commented, 'A lot of water has flowed under the bridge since Streeter'. Normally a gentle and courteous speaker, Austin could be sharp when faced with widespread scholarly fashion. Streeter had written his book in 1924, and it had established a generally accepted solution to the problem of the relation between the Gospels: Austin had written a critique of Streeter which was to be published in 1955, and he regarded Streeter's solution as part of what he called 'institutionalized folly'. I will return to Streeter in Chapter 13. Another widespread fashion of the time was a movement called Form Criticism, which Austin regarded as misguided. A leading exponent of this school was Dennis Nineham, whose commentary on St Mark was widely praised. Some years later Nineham put in for a higher Oxford degree, and Austin was appointed one of his examiners in a public hearing. To one of Austin's questions Nineham objected, 'But that would be to question the whole basis of Form Criticism'. Austin replied, 'And that would be to touch the Ark of the Covenant, wouldn't it?'

Austin raised a point of real difficulty for me. I should be studying for a BA in Theology, and there were a number of set papers, such as Old and New Testament. But there was also one paper which I could choose: I could take it either in Hebrew or in Philosophy. Austin recommended the Hebrew option: the Church needed Hebraists. I was reluctant to go against this advice, but Austin was not himself a Hebrew scholar, and I had crossed the world to study with him as a philosopher. So I plumped for the philosophy paper. This had considerable benefits for me in later life, when I came to lecture in Birmingham on the philosophy of religion; but I missed the Hebrew. It was twenty years before I had a chance to study the language, and I was to write a number of books on the Hebrew Bible, which would have been easier if I had studied the language from earlier years.

Austin was a successful Chaplain at Trinity. The College had an unfortunate tradition of public-schoolboys with snobbish and racist attitudes; but under Austin's influence, out of 170 undergraduates 16 were ordinands—if I were included, 10%. Evenings in the Chaplain's room were always interesting, when we came, as he said, 'to hear my lion roar', that is, to listen to an invited speaker. He was quite candid with us: after an evening discussing miracles, we asked him if he himself had ever performed a miracle. He said reluctantly, 'I did once feel moved to pray for a tramp who was dying, and in the inscrutable wisdom of God he recovered briefly, before dying a few weeks later'. Austin was an exciting preacher. He delivered his sermons at Evensong in a quiet unemotional voice; but they were full of deep thinking, and often poetically expressed. The Prayer Book provides that there should be a sermon at the Eucharist; and Austin developed the habit of drafting beautiful two-minute addresses, to which we listened spellbound. Some years later he received an unwelcome letter from the Inland Revenue demanding several years' back payments of income tax. He had no savings to cover this and felt driven to earn some money quickly. So he sent his Eucharist sermons to a publisher, and they appeared as *The Crown of the Year,* combining the two purposes of edification and debt-repayment. These addresses were models of conciseness and profundity, poetically expressed.

The Chapel community provided me with a ready circle of friends. The closest of these was Murray Sanderson, a man of great devotion, but, as the Apostle says, 'his zeal was not always according to knowledge'. Murray rose at 5.30 a.m. to pray, and breakfasted on bread and margarine, lest he be corrupted by the college fleshpots. I admired this, and was unfortunately impressed by a rule for sleep ascribed to Napoleon: 'six hours for a man, seven hours for a woman, eight hours for a fool'. Six hours was not enough for me, but Nature soon took her revenge. I used to go to sleep during the lectures of I.T. Ramsey, a renowned philosopher of religion. The class was small and he could not avoid seeing my head down on the desk; as he went out, on one occasion, he deposited a copy of the notes of his lecture beside me. Fortunately I drew the line at margarine, and did not ruin my health with an inferior diet. Murray was not destined to be a parson, but he aspired to a higher level of self-dedication. His family were wealthy; his father was the Manager of the White Star shipping line at Liverpool, whence the Titanic sailed on her fateful voyage. Murray felt his calling was to bring a more humane form of industrialization to sub-Saharan Africa, and he sold most of his assets in order to fund this endeavour. He built factories, first to make women's underclothes, later to make mowers, and in time he planted groves of macadamia nut-trees. He paid good wages and made his workers shareholders in the enterprises. For a time his factories went well; but eventually a combination of national inflation and corruption made it impossible for him to do business, and in the end his high ambitions were largely disappointed.

Back in Oxford, just before term started in October 1952, on my way to visit a mutual friend for tea, I first saw Clare Gardner, who had come out to meet me in the gardens of Lady Margaret Hall. Our hostess was not quite ready for us, and we walked round that garden, talking non-stop, and I at once felt strongly drawn to her. She had known who I was, as she used to attend St Mary's Church, and her interest in Christianity was keen and immediate; she had been prepared for Confirmation in June that year by the Vicar Roy Lee. But I hesitated for a while before committing myself, wondering whether I had some vocation to be a missionary, in which case a wife and family might present problems. But I actually felt no clear calling in this direction, and in fact marriage has never provided any obstacle to my life's work. I have also to say that Clare's charms were a very strong influence. Relations with her family were not entirely easy, but we were finally married on 7 August, after Clare graduated, at her village church in Tattenhall near Chester.

I enjoyed my studies, and from the first found the New Testament fascinating. There was a New Testament prize, the Hall Houghton, which I went in for and won. It was, however, easy to be over-impressed by Austin. I found his books, *A Study in St Mark* and *A Rebirth of Images,* intoxicating, and in the end this was too much of a good thing. When I came to write my Final exam papers Austin expected me to get a First, but in fact I had to be content with a Second. Years later, Christopher Evans, who had been Chairman of the examiners, told Clare at a party that my papers had been so full of Austin's ideas that they thought I had no originality, and so withheld the First; but he had soon realized how wrong they had been and said he had felt guilty ever since! He made handsome amends, however, by inviting me on the occasion of his seventieth birthday to join with him in a public discussion of my work. At the time Clare and I were disappointed, of course, but my mother stoutly declared that, having told all her Bridge friends that I had got a First, she was not going to disillusion them now!

Chapter 5

SALFORD

R.O. had written to his one-time curate of Newcastle days, Billy Greer, now Bishop of Manchester, asking him to find me a job. Always short of clergy, Billy was pleased to accede, and found me a curacy in Salford, a grimy city to the west of Manchester. In view of my later career as a scholar, one might wonder that I did not at this stage try to continue at Oxford and write a doctorate. Probably my Second would have precluded this, but in any case I had no wish to tread this path. I had set my hand to the pastoral plough and did not wish to turn back. Austin was very discouraging about doctorates: many of those who did them became depressed and lonely and lacked an interest in what they were writing about. I was deeply suspicious of what looked like an easier option leading to a comfortable life in a college. So in September 1953 I thumbed a lift from Essex to Salford, where I met my new Vicar, John McClintock. Jock, as we called him, was Vicar of St Thomas', Pendleton, with its daughter church St Anne's, Brindle Heath. Jock was by no means of the same spiritual calibre as those who had been my mentors hitherto. He was an Irishman, of the old Protestant Ascendancy, and treated the parishioners as if they were his tenants in County Sligo. He had won the MC as a Chaplain in the War, and this background lent to his manner of dealing with people a slight military timbre, which was not always very acceptable. He had married somewhat late in life, Hester, who came from a rather upper-crust Gloucestershire family, and they had three small children. Hester had an even more superior attitude to the Salford people than her husband, and also she did not draw a clear distinction between a curate and a servant. There was a senior curate, Robert Douglas, a charming and hardworking man with a good sense of humour, which he needed. He was given responsibility for much of the St Thomas' parish: there was a fine Waterloo church built about 1834, though blackened since with Salford soot; St Anne's was a smaller, undistinguished modern church down in the valley, and I was given a pretty free hand in that area, which suited me fine. Clare and I were given a house, St Anne's Vicarage, to live in, which was nearly a mile up the Bolton Road. This had the advantage of being higher than the parish, and enjoyed clearer air, but I became only too familiar with the steep climb on my bicycle at the end of the day.

Jock held a number of implausible theories; one of these was that as the Church was short of clergy as much money as possible should be invested in machines. So the Vicarage was full of modern devices: there was a floor-polisher, and an amplifier which enabled one to continue a telephone conversation from the far end of the room while consulting one's filing cabinet. He had a phut-phut machine, a small petrol engine attached to the back wheel of his bicycle to provide extra power going up the Salford inclines. Some of these machines did not in fact save the time of the clergy. There was a Staff meeting in the Vicarage at 9.30 on Monday mornings, but it never actually began till 10.00 because Jock was polishing the floor. The meeting closed about 12.30 with lunch in the Vicarage kitchen; after which the curates were expected to assist with the washing-up. This was a disgusting procedure. Among the machines which Jock bought there was not included one to heat the water adequately. So Hester presided over a bowl of luke-warm water in which floated large islands of grease. We were supplied with drying-up towels to complete the process. These were already grey before we used them, and inevitably much of the fat which still adhered to the plates was transferred to the cloths, causing them to stink and to be transferred onto further plates and cutlery. Robert had the temerity to pass back one spoon heavily encrusted with grease for a second wash, and was reprimanded for being so fussy. Hester had married at 39 and had had her three children within five years. She was not born to life in an industrial parish and lacked the pliability to master an alien environment.

Clare had been pregnant when we arrived in Salford. An old friend of her family's, an obstetrician called Jack Wigley, offered to look after her when the time came; but he worked in Chester. In January of 1955 it was found that we were expecting twins, but unfortunately by February Clare had developed the symptoms of toxaemia and had to be admitted to Chester City Hospital. It was a great comfort to feel that my wife was in the best possible hands; but the arrangement did have its downside. Two or three times a week I made the journey to visit her, going by bus into Manchester, by train to Chester, and again by bus out to the hospital. The journey was often anxious: I had to synchronize the long bus journey with the Manchester train, and with a busy timetable I had to run the time close. Sometimes I stayed overnight at Clare's parents' home, and then I had also to take our cat, Quince. I would put him into a wicker 'Hong Kong' basket. On one occasion I had to chase the train as it was

leaving the platform; I threw the basket into the open door, and jumped
in myself behind it. Once I was so tired that I fell asleep on the homeward
journey, and like the lady who read *Everybody's* in the advertisement,
I got carried on to Crewe. In all the weeks Clare was in hospital I never
missed a visit. The twins were born, two girls, on Easter Eve, 9 April, and
so I was able to make this happy announcement at the Easter service at
St Anne's the following day.

May was an eventful month. On the twentieth, Ascension Day, Clare
came home to our vicarage, after a short stay at her parents' home. She
had gone into hospital on Shrove Tuesday, so her progress followed the
pattern of the Church's liturgical year. At about the same time, the Bishop
offered Robert Douglas the post of Vicar of Worsley. In his humility, or
folly, Robert consulted Jock as to whether he should accept; and was
told that he should decline as he was not mature enough to have his own
church. I think that this advice was in part due to the influence of Hester,
who never concealed her low opinion of Robert. I particularly resented
this as although she had a low opinion of curates in general she treated
me slightly better, perhaps because I had been to Eton. Fortunately
Robert decided to disregard the advice: not only was he fully experienced
enough to run a church of his own, but he also needed the position in
order to get married to an attractive fiancée who had already had to wait
too long. Only a few days after Clare's homecoming, Robert and I were
saying Evensong together in St Thomas' Church; it was our custom for
the three of us clergy to do this together, but Jock was often late, and we
had started without him. Suddenly one of the choir-girls ran in to the
church crying out that the Vicar had been run over. Jock's enthusiasm for
machines had been his undoing. The moped wobbled as he tried to start
it at the traffic lights, and he was thrown in the path of an oncoming lorry,
which killed him instantly. It is nice that the last thing I remember him
doing was cycling up to our house with a handsome bunch of carnations
to greet Clare and the babies on their return. I took the first part of the
funeral in St Anne's, and as I escorted the coffin up the road to St Thomas',
there were people standing on both sides of the street. Jock had been
Vicar of St Anne's for years before he had also taken over St Thomas'; he
had been Chairman of Governors at both the St Anne's Church Schools;
he had baptized, married, and buried people from many families in the
area, and, despite his military manners, had inspired a certain degree of
affection. These people joined the choir in singing the familiar words,
'Onward Christian soldiers' as we went past.

Within the course of two weeks the parishes had lost their Vicar and
their senior curate, and the Bishop was reduced to asking the surviving

staff member, that is me, to assume responsibility for the two parishes during the interregnum. This was to mean a lot of work. But first, there was a fulfilling of a duty which Jock had laid on me, the CLB. Before my time he had introduced the Church Lads' Brigade at St Anne's as a suitable youth club, and had persuaded four young men from the congregation to act as its officers. When I arrived I was instructed to take command of this little unit, an unwelcome duty for the most unmilitary of men. The CLB was a recipe for despair. There were only two activities: one was drill, as uninspiring to the boys as to the officers, and the other was carpentry. Someone had produced an old fallen tree, and a plane was provided with which to turn this into something constructive. But the task was impractical, and the repeated attempts week after week were deeply depressing. In the first flush of commonsense I suggested to the officers that we officers should end the evenings with a visit to the pub. This did a lot for morale, and in the course of time I suggested to them that we might take the lads away for a camp. I had no business to do this as I had no experience of camping, nor any training, and unbeknownst to me the CLB forbade any such activity without such qualifications. At least I had had the sense to postpone the exercise till the summer, and the project was planned for Whit Week when there was a school holiday. This then happened almost immediately after Jock's death. I took the officers and a senior boy, George, to find a good camping site. I knew that there was suitable moorland in Derbyshire, and that two necessities were a stream and some dead wood for a fire, and we soon found what we were looking for. It did not occur to me that the land might belong to somebody, and at any moment an angry farmer might arrive to turn us off.

I prepared the boys with a talk on the importance of adequate blankets for the night, and on the mysteries of latrines. We were able to hire two tents, and the officers carried these up the hillside, while I filled my rucksack with a large weight of tinned provisions, far more than I could easily carry. But all went well. The tents were erected and the fire built; the boys gathered contentedly around it and sang, and the officers succeeded in cooking sausages on long toasting forks, and baked beans, which were appreciated. Unwisely I decided that the boys should sleep in one tent and the officers in another. But George who was a big-mouth had boasted that he had been to the campsite, and it was 'no bloody good'; and as soon as the boys were settled in their sleeping bags, there arose a derisive chorus of 'Bin to the campsaat, norr blooody good'. This was repeated about two hundred times, and on each occasion drew the satisfying response, 'Shoot oop, or Ar'll beat yer moosh in'. In fact no mooshes were beaten in, but then nor did anybody get any sleep for two hours. About four in the morning the cold had become severe, and a fat boy called Crockett was pushed out and stumbled into the officers' tent to take refuge. A little while later, while it was still dark, the boys all got up to resurrect the fire and warm themselves. We were fortunate to eat breakfast, break camp without further incident, and return safely to Salford. The incident was typical of my naïve willingness to undertake tasks for which I was not fitted, and I was lucky to have escaped from it relatively unscathed.

I returned to my vicarage to give what help I could to Clare, who was heroically coping with the ceaseless demands of multiple motherhood. One particular complication was that, owing to a difficult birth, and a week in an incubator, Cathy needed to be fed by bottle, whereas Lizzie was breastfed. These two things could not be done at the same time, and so I came in and helped by feeding Cathy three times a day. In those days there were no disposable nappies, and each day Clare was washing thirty nappies and putting them out on the line to dry; they came in covered in smuts from the dirty air. As curate-in-charge I was responsible for Sunday services in both churches: 8.0 a.m. Communion at St Anne's; 9.15 Communion at St Thomas'; 10.30 Mattins at St Anne's; 2.30 Sunday School; 6.30 Evensong. For eight months I had no breakfast on Sundays. On weekdays there were occasional funerals, and marriage interviews; both churches had meetings of their Church Councils; there were Confirmation classes; and I introduced Sunday School teachers' preparation classes, which were a success, especially when Clare ended the meetings by serving baked beans on toast for everybody.

In addition to all this, I was involved in some battles. A high point in the parish each year was the Bishop's visit for Confirmation. I prepared the candidates, mostly those leaving the Sunday School, with a course of eight talks; I called on the parents of each candidate and explained that I could present only those who had attended the classes and come once a week to church. One thirteen-year-old called Carol came only very irregularly to the classes, and not at all to church, so I called to tell her mother that I could not include her name. She was not prepared to take No from a mere curate-in-charge, and sought the help of Mr Snape, the Vicar of the neighbouring church of St Paul, Paddington. I would not have known of this but for the clergy breakfast, which was attended once a month by the local clergy. At this I happened to overhear the Rural Dean telling Snape that he had included the extra name on the Confirmation list. When I was sure that this was the Carol from my parish, I wrote a piece of English prose to the Bishop, asking how far my authority ran. The Bishop summoned me and Snape to discuss the matter, and in a tactful way firmly took my side. At the end of the meeting Snape said to him that he thought the time had come for him to retire.

A few days later I was faced with a crisis that I had been fearing, that is, a rift between the two church communities. The people at St Anne's were very sensitive about relations with the bigger church, St Thomas', and there was always danger of umbrage being taken at casual remarks. (An instance of this sensitivity was to occur some months later, when the new Vicar bought a minibus to transport the parishioners; seeing a group of St Anne's mothers awaiting a bus, he drew in to offer them a lift, and was greeted with the sturdily independent response, 'We're not going in St Thomas' booss'). The crisis arose at a meeting of St Thomas' Parish Church Council, where an arrogant young man called Joplin made some offensive remarks about Annie Wylie, a likeable if somewhat eccentric pillar of St Anne's. I knew that once the rumour of this was spread abroad, there would be strong resentment in St Anne's, so I called on Joplin, and asked him to withdraw his remarks. When he refused I pressed him, and as it became evident that he was not going to retract I said that he must do so or I should excommunicate him! Excommunication is a serious matter, and I was not too sure of my ground; so I went home quickly, and looked up in the Prayer Book to see what the rules were for such an action. The matter was set out quite clearly: in such cases the action must be reported to the Bishop within a fortnight. The last thing I wanted was a second interview with the Bishop so soon after the one with Mr Snape, and this time luck was on my side. There was a sensible man called Ike Chapman, a Reader at St Anne's; when he heard what had happened, he went independently and spoke to Joplin, persuading him to come down to the church and shake Annie Wylie's hand. He asked me to be there too, and the reconciliation was achieved, much to the relief of all.

Early in the New Year I was relieved to hear that the interregnum was over and a new Vicar was coming. He was a Welshman called Deas, and the contrast between the Deases and the McClintocks could hardly have been stronger. They were an unassuming couple, with five children; Deas was sensible, and they were hospitable and soon made excellent relations with the parishes, and also with me. And far from treating me as the most junior of curates, he preferred to address me as Mr Goulder, although I would have been quite happy with Michael.

Chapter 6

St Luke and Genesis

With Deas' arrival I was able to return to the long-unfamiliar experience of a little leisure; and went back to my first love, the study of the New Testament. We had been reading the Christmas stories from Luke's Gospel in church, and I began where Luke does, with the marvellous birth of John the Baptist. John's father and mother, Zechariah and Elizabeth, were too old to have children, and God sent an angel to Zechariah with the promise of a son of destiny, a promise which Zechariah does not believe. Other people had noticed that there is a very similar story in the book of Genesis: Abraham and his wife Sarah are too old to have children and God sends an angel to promise Abraham the birth of a son of destiny, Isaac, a promise which Abraham too does not believe. I noticed several things about this. Not only were the stories themselves very similar, but so also were the words in which they were told. The Old Testament was written in Hebrew, but about 300 BCE, some Jews in Alexandria translated it into their language, which was Greek. The need to give authority to this translation gave rise to a legend that 70 Jewish elders had sat down separately and had miraculously produced identical versions. This translation then came to be called the Septuagint (from the Latin for seventy), often abbreviated to LXX. This translation became the Bible of the early Church, which included St Luke himself, and it is striking that Luke's Gospel contains phrases identical to those in the LXX, such as 'they were advanced in days', where one would naturally say 'they were old'. So it began to look as if the story was not so much a record of a true experience of Zechariah, but rather one composed by Luke himself on the pattern of the Abraham/Isaac story.

This surmise was confirmed by two further features. A little further on Mary, who is even more marvellously to be the virgin mother of Christ, comes to visit Elizabeth, her cousin, and when Elizabeth sees her the baby John leaps in her womb in recognition of his Lord. This is again similar to the Genesis story, where Rebekah is pregnant with the two boys Esau and Jacob and the children leap in her womb, symbolising that the older, Esau, will serve the younger, Jacob, who is again the child of destiny. The more I went over the text the more I felt could be explained from the Old Testament: why Zechariah was a priest, for example, why he was struck dumb for his unbelief, and even the names Zechariah, Elizabeth, Anna, and Gabriel. The conclusion seemed clear: the whole story about both John's and Jesus' births were not so much historical, as compositions by St Luke woven from 'types' in the Old Testament. He felt that the Old Testament was a prophecy of what was to happen in the New, partly prophesied in word and partly foreshadowed in narrative. I wrote out a draft article and sent it to Murray Sanderson. He replied enthusiastically, making some helpful criticisms and adding a few suggestions of his own. I then rewrote the article and sent it to Austin to ask his opinion. To my pleasure he replied positively, though he was cautious about dismissing tradition entirely; and recommended that I send it to Professor Hedley Sparks, the editor of *The Journal of Theological Studies*, the foremost English journal. He accepted it, and it was published in April 1957 under the title, 'St Luke's Genesis', by Murray and myself.

Naturally I was proud to see my name among the contributors listed on the prestigious light blue cover of the *JTS*; and I sat down to await seeing references to it among the footnotes of the learned with suitable respectful comments. In fact the reception of my article was slightly different. A few months after its publication, Dr Cross, a Canon of Christ Church, Oxford, announced a conference to help clergy and ministers in pastoral work to keep up with University thinking about the New Testament. I thought I would like to go to this, and the Bishop kindly agreed to fund my doing so. I travelled with a fellow clergyman, Rex Hartley, and sat with him for the opening session. To my amazement this was announced as a lecture on 'Recent work on Luke 1–2'; I was to have my work discussed before an audience of several hundreds. The speaker was a Scottish Professor, Robin Wilson, of St Andrews. He began with a discussion of articles by two scholars, Turner and Winter, who were interested in Luke's having used some Hebrew documents from John the Baptist's family. I sat rather restlessly waiting for him to come to the real substance of the topic, my own article, but to my surprise this was delayed almost indefinitely. Wilson had a rather ponderous sense of humour and his text was lightened only by a few not very funny jokes; finally in the fifty-eighth minute he paused, and in a new, sarcastic voice, said, 'However, there has recently been a different approach by M.D. Goulder and M.L. Sanderson...' He gave a digest of our conclusions in two sentences, and dismissed them with the words 'Typology run riot!' I felt like the man in the Bateman cartoons who attends a function dressed in the wrong clothes, and everyone in the room stares at him. But I need not have worried. The lecture had been very boring and almost everyone was asleep; even Rex, sitting next to me, had nodded off, and had no idea that I had been mentioned.

My disappointment was due in large part to my inexperience. I had supposed that scholars were dedicated to the pursuit of truth, wherever that might lead, and that new ideas would always be welcome. This however is only partly true. Before new ideas come, scholars have reached a consensus, and their position as authorities depends upon their agreeing with that consensus. Their teachers, whom they normally honoured, had taught them the consensus; they had written their books assuming it, and they had often helped to develop it themselves. They were not at all likely, therefore, to think that they and their fellow experts had been wrong, and that a new scholar, of whom they had not heard, was in a position to put them right. But there is another problem: most scholars of the New Testament have religious loyalties: they want the text to be orthodox, or historical, or preachable, or relevant. So any new interpretation which does not fulfil these conditions is not likely to be approved.

I had to wait nearly twenty years for my vindication. My friend John Sweet had proposed me for membership of the SNTS, the international Society of New Testament Studies. This society comprised almost all the leading NT scholars in the world. It was originally an Anglo-European society, but from the seventies meetings were held in America too. Universities would take it in turns to host the Society's meeting in August each year, and in 1976 the Meeting was held at Duke University, Durham, North Carolina. It was traditional for the Committee to invite a speaker from the host community and on this occasion they had asked Father Raymond Brown, a distinguished liberal Roman Catholic scholar. Raymond was to deliver a paper on the same theme that Robin Wilson had taken at Oxford back in 1958, and the audience were expectant before the lecture began: it was by now widely accepted that Luke 1–2 was much indebted to types and prophecies in the Old Testament; but Brown was a faithful Catholic, and could hardly come to the same sceptical conclusions as I had about the historicity of the birth narratives. At first his lecture followed my article step by step: he cited most of the passages which I had used, and referred to me by name; he thought I had gone too far in trying to explain the names, and tried to raise a laugh at my expense, but to my relief nobody responded. Eventually he turned to the crucial question of history. How much then of these two chapters could we think was historical? Three things, he answered:

John's parents really were called Zechariah and Elizabeth; his father really was a priest; and Jesus' mother Mary was a virgin at the time of the conception. When he had finished Barnabas Lindars, an Anglican Franciscan, sitting next to me, rose to ask the first question: 'You have cited a good number of passages from the Old Testament. But you did not mention Isaiah chapter 7 verse 14'. This verse reads, 'Behold a virgin shall conceive and bring forth a child...' Raymond replied weakly, 'I do not think that Luke had noticed that text'. I felt doubly vindicated by this occasion. The link between the birth narratives and Old Testament passages, like the Abraham/Isaac passage, which I had argued for in my article, were now being publicly approved, and my name cited in connection with them. But also I felt vindicated over my conclusion. It was scandalous to suggest that these narratives were not historical, but I had been bold enough to draw the obvious inference. Raymond however looked as if he had ducked the clear but unwelcome conclusion. Where the parallels in the Old Testament to a story in Luke did not threaten a cherished belief, Raymond was happy to accept that Luke had inferred the stories from the OT texts, without having evidence that they were actually historical; but the Isaiah text would imply that Luke had also inferred the Virgin Birth, and this was a cherished belief which he was not willing to abandon. There are many places not only in Luke 1–2, but throughout the Gospel and Acts, where Luke shows a close knowledge of Isaiah's prophecy, and it was just special pleading to suggest that he had not noticed Isa. 7.14. This was only the first of many occasions in which I came to find that the holding of religious belief proved an obstacle to the impartial evaluation of evidence.

Chapter 7

St Christopher's, Withington

This incident took place in 1976; but by this time I was no longer in Salford. A few months after Deas's arrival, the Bishop offered me the position of Rector of St Christopher's Church, Withington, in South Manchester. I was to be six years there, and they were not the most happy of my life. The parish consisted of a large Council estate built in the Thirties, and those who lived in it had been there since then, and were generally about 55 years old, with children in their teens. The previous incumbent had been a controversial figure, and the Church Council was bitterly divided between those who had supported him from loyalty, like the churchwardens, and Sam Beagles, the Treasurer, who had pressed for him to leave the parish. The tensions he had aroused did not disappear with his departure, and for many months every discussion on the PCC ended with a vote splitting 8/9 or 9/8. A particular cause of dissension was the Parish Hall. The church was a huge brick construction surmounted by a blue neon cross, commanding a view down the drive to Princess Parkway. To its left as you emerged was the handsome seven-bedroom Rectory, which was to be our home. To its right was an empty piece of ground intended as the site of a fine Hall to balance the Rectory. Unfortunately this hope had suffered the fate of many church building schemes: each year the Treasurer set aside enough money to add ten percent to the fund, and each year the cost of building rose by twenty percent. The previous Rector had hoped to resolve the dilemma by opting for a cheap prefabricated hall; while Beagles would not be content without a dignified, brick building to complete the group. It took some years before this problem was resolved.

I was unlucky in that my arrival in the parish happened to coincide with an unfortunate moment in our country's history. I came in August 1956, and at once visited the parish organizations: the Mothers' Union, the 'Fellowship', which was in fact a dancing club for older people, the Youth Club, and—to my surprise—the Ex-Servicemen's Association. The last was in reality a billiards club, and when I inquired if they ever went to church, I was assured that they did so indeed, on Remembrance Sunday: 'Sgt-Major Bishop falls us in Minehead Avenue, and we march to church, where you read the Roll of the Fallen'. The Suez Crisis developed at the end of October. Egypt was one of the poorest countries in the world, with one natural advantage, the Canal. With its constant stream of boats passing through this could have provided fees enough materially to improve the lot of the people. But the Canal had been built eighty years earlier by a French engineer, and most of the shares had been bought for Britain by Disraeli in 1872: so the preponderance of the fees was going to Britain and France. There had recently been a coup in Egypt, and General Nasser had overthrown the old corrupt monarchy. He now announced his intention of nationalising, i.e. purloining the Canal. When he did so this was a severe humiliation for Britain; and Anthony Eden, the Prime Minister, supported by Harold Macmillan, decided to collude with the French and the Israelis in attacking Egypt so as to regain the Canal. There was much rhetoric about little Hitlers and Nasser's thumb on our windpipe, but the fact was that British forces were fighting in Egypt on 11 November 1956. It was my task to say something from the pulpit, and I had no doubt what I should say. Our action was one of flagrant imperialistic aggression, and it was precisely against such actions that we had fought the Second World War: we needed a new Government. The prophet Amos would not have been ashamed of my sermon. Such, however, was by no means the mood of the congregation; as Mr Scott, the Churchwarden, put it, the proper attitude is, 'My country, right or wrong'. I went to discuss the issue with the Ex-Servicemen the following Friday. I asked them to say what they thought, and Sgt-Major Bishop said, 'There was an officer sitting next to me. After the service he said, 'Your parson doesn't know his job'. I said, 'He ought to: he's been to University". Dear Mr Bishop: blessed are the pure in heart. This seemingly minor episode was actually the first of many occasions when the clash of my views with those of Mr Scott caused a souring of the atmosphere.

In 1957 an event took place which was to shock many people and was important for my own religious belief. The Manchester United football team set off from Munich to fly back to England; it was a cold night, and there was ice frozen onto the wings, and the plane crashed after take-off, killing almost everyone on board. The news caused desolation in Manchester, and as the procession conveying the bodies drove up Princess Parkway from Ringway Airport, the streets were lined with mourners on both sides. Inevitably I had to make some comment in my sermon the following Sunday. This event revealed an unpleasant chasm in my theology. Austin Farrer believed in an active God, guiding human affairs. He wrote in *Faith and Speculation:* 'The hearts of kings are in His rule and governance, and He turneth them as seemeth best to His godly wisdom'. So I had been used to explaining the blessings of life as evidence of divine Providence; but now that a disaster had occurred, I naturally said that it was human responsibility to make sure there was no ice weighing down the wings of an aeroplane. This was uncomfortably like having it both ways, and was the beginning of a loss of confidence in my theological message.

The following year brought a more pleasant surprise. I had a phone call from Wilf Wilkinson, the Vicar of Wythenshawe, to say that he had managed to raise promises of £60,000, which would be enough to build his new church; he was phoning every incumbent in the diocese, to let them know, and to invite them to a reception in a hotel. Baythorpe and Scott, my two Wardens, and Beagles the Treasurer, attended this reception with me; Wilkinson introduced representatives of the Wells organization, who explained how the money had been raised. The entire parish had been invited to an enormous Dinner, where the needs of the church were explained, and it was said that the men of the church would be calling in the following weeks to solicit pledges of worthy amounts of money. The officers from St Christopher's were much impressed by this, but they baulked at the considerable fee which the Wells people were asking. They felt that the idea was good, and we could manage it ourselves on a DIY basis. I was alarmed myself at the responsibility I should be undertaking if I had to train the various groups without the experience that the professionals would have supplied; but I was unwilling to frustrate the enthusiasm for positive action, shown especially by Scott and Beagles. Following the old division, Baythorpe was more sceptical, and referred to the project as 'commercialising Christ'.

The PCC voted to proceed with the Wells scheme, but without professional assistance; so we set out on a project requiring formidable organization. First, the parish was divided into streets, and the women of the church were asked to call on each house in their district, to let people know of the Dinner and to ask if they would like to attend. Some weeks later those who had shown interest were presented with a nicely printed card on which their name had been written; and the acceptances now gave us an idea of how much transport would be needed. There was a small team of 'Queen Bees' keeping an oversight of the whole endeavour; the take-up was encouragingly large, and we ordered twenty-four double-decker buses. The women took responsibility for shepherding their flocks onto the buses, for seeing them seated at the Dinner, and for escorting them safely home afterwards. A venue was selected at the Urmston Baths, which were covered over in winter. We found a caterer who would provide a good menu at eight shillings and sixpence per head, which was quite a lot of money for those days. The church was paying for the whole evening, so it was a considerable investment to be risking, and we were fortunate that the meal turned out to be generally appreciated. The occasion had its zany aspects. The Bishop had been invited, and came resplendent in his Episcopal purple. The ladies of the church came in their finery; Clare was decked in Auntie Peggy's green and gold brocade. Mrs Crow had secured the services of a Welsh tenor, who sang a wildly unsuitable number, 'Questa o quella', from Rigoletto, a song in praise of sexual licence; fortunately most of the audience would have been none the wiser. After the meal the Bishop spoke, and then I gave the keynote address: I said that Christians should show their gratitude to God by supporting the Church worthily. St Christopher's had an income of £17 a week, and could not manage if people only gave sixpence or a shilling. Our team of men would call on each house over the next five weeks, and would ask those who had attended the Dinner to make a pledge of what they would give in future. At the end of this time I would ring the church bell the number of times that pounds a week had been promised.

The most tricky part of the whole business was the training of the men's team, because everything depended on their approach being acceptable. This was difficult for me as I did not have the help of the experienced Wells people, but had to do the best I could. In fact the operation went very well; when the five weeks were over I was able to ring the church bell seventy-one times. This result exceeded our highest hopes, and effectively solved our financial problems over the years to come.

Immediately we were able to commission an architect to draw up plans for the long-awaited Parish Hall. He designed an attractive building which was built over the next year and cost £26,000. There was a porch, a kitchen, lavatories, and a large hall with a stage and polished wood floor. There was ample seating for meetings, plays, etc., and, later, services; and the floor was convenient for what our children called the 'dafty dancing' by the old people. The Hall proved to be an even bigger asset than we had expected. All the time that I was there we had anxieties over the church's structure: cracks appeared in the brickwork, and there were constant leaks from the flat roof, which handymen from the congregation tried in vain to stem with coats of tar. Some time after my departure the cracks grew worse, and the architect declared the building unsafe, and it was then demolished. The services could then be transferred to the Hall, and in many ways this was an improvement. There was always difficulty heating the church; people used to shiver and grumble, and Baythorpe would try to deceive them by putting his thumb on the thermometer at the back of the church, thus raising its temperature. Also the church had a bad echo, which was a problem for the preacher. But above all it had been built to seat 500, but the congregation was rarely more than 150 even at Christmas; most of these sat in the back, in the Anglican manner, thus creating a huge vacuum in the middle of the church. By contrast the Hall was comfortably warm and had good acoustics, and was just the right size.

During the Dinner campaign life was hectic indeed; but from the beginning both Clare and I worked very hard. I was up each morning in time to ring the church bell for Morning Prayer at 7.00; I read, and wrote—sermons, articles for the parish paper, later more learned articles. After lunch I would cycle off to visit the sick and elderly. There was Evensong at 6.0 p.m., followed by opportunity for interviews. Then in the evening I normally visited four or five homes, when there were men about, who would have been at work during the day. There were about eight thousand people in the parish, and I attempted to visit everybody; I was always hoping to persuade adults to be Confirmed, as a means of bringing them into the Church. Some evenings there were Confirmation classes or marriage-preparation classes, or the Youth Club or other organizations. Our garden consisted of a lawn giving onto a shrubbery; the latter was dominated by two large crab-apple trees, which were covered in scarlet fruit. The year we came, there was a Michaelmas Fair, and Clare turned to and made 123 lbs of crab-apple jelly, which sold like hot cakes. The money was given to the Congregational Stall, which caused some resentment from the Mothers' Union, which had always topped the takings in earlier years. This was an example of an attitude in the church that led Clare to realize how different was the 'Christianity' in Withington from what she had been so inspired by in Oxford, and to begin to lose confidence in her faith.

But Clare's contribution was often in the form of hospitality in the Rectory. Before our time the PCC meetings had been held in the church vestry, but we thought it would improve the atmosphere if we invited the members to the Rectory. This was not, however, a success, even when on one occasion Clare made some little cakes for the tea interval, and we felt very discouraged. We comforted ourselves by bringing down Lizzie, who was wakeful, at 10.00 p.m., and feeding her on the left-over cakes. Bible study and other meetings were also held in our house. Soon after our coming, I had a letter from a vicar in Jersey, asking me to keep an eye on a girl called Vicky, who had come to work as an au pair in the parish. I invited Vicky to join the Youth Club, and it soon became clear that she was not happy with her family; so we offered her a home with us while she looked for another job. I took her to an interview at the Didsbury Cotton Research Institute, and when she got the job Clare suggested that she stayed on with us and helped a little with the children. Vicky turned out to be a long-term guest; she was helpful, and good with the children, but at times could be moody and appear disaffected. After about eighteen months we felt she should find somewhere else; but the landlord of the place she found wanted more than just the rent, and the police soon brought her back to us for sanctuary, along with another girl, whom we also reluctantly accepted. So we had them for another year.

There were other occasional guests. One night I came home to find Clare talking to a stranger who told me he was a clergyman of the Church of Ireland. We offered him a bed for the night, but when he joined me for Morning Prayer, it became clear that he was unfamiliar with the service. We asked him to sign our visitors' book, but he couldn't write, and we realized we had been taken in. I checked on his credentials, and was told that he was an imposter who had been using a real clergyman's name for many months. We also tried to improve race relations in the parish by asking people to entertain Anglicans from Africa over a weekend. We ourselves welcomed for a longer period a Nigerian lady, Mrs Adelogbe, who was in Manchester for a course on teaching deaf children. This was not a success. She did not turn up on time to meals which Clare had specially prepared; at other times she would take over the kitchen when Clare had said she needed to be there herself, and would cook strong-smelling African stews. One night when I was away she asked Clare to call her at 7.00 a.m. so she could attend a lecture in Bolton. Clare had been up all night with one of the children, and it was the last straw when, on being called a second time, Mrs Adelogbe said she had decided not to go after all. This was the end of her visit.

Chapter 8

THE LORD'S PRAYER

When the Dinner campaign was over, I again had a little leisure, and went back to my study of St Luke. I soon became interested in the Lord's Prayer, which presents problems. The Prayer is not mentioned in Mark's Gospel; and this is the more curious, because Mark records a saying of Jesus, 'When you pray, forgive if you have anything against anybody, that your heavenly Father may forgive you your trespasses'. The version of the Prayer nearest to what most Christians know by heart is found in Matthew's Gospel. A close translation from the Greek would read: 'Our father in heaven, Hallowed be thy name; Thy kingdom come; Thy will be done, On earth as in heaven. Give us today our bread for the coming day; And forgive us our debts, as we forgive our debtors. And bring us not into temptation, but deliver us from the evil one'. Luke has a somewhat shorter version: 'Father, Hallowed be thy name; Thy kingdom come; Thy will be done. Give us each day our bread for the coming day. And forgive us our sins, for we ourselves forgive everyone indebted to us. And bring us not into temptation'.

It is very surprising that Mark should have left the Prayer out, after including Jesus' teaching on prayer and forgiveness. An explanation for this occurred to me. Although this is the only direct teaching on prayer in Mark, Jesus does in a way teach the disciples indirectly by his own prayer in Gethsemane. It is noticeable how many of the sentences in Gethsemane recur in Matthew's Lord's Prayer: *Father; Not my will but thine be done; Watch and pray that you enter not into temptation*. It looks as if Matthew has thought to himself, 'Christians need a prayer which they can say regularly; I could compose an ideal Prayer of Jesus by combining his Gethsemane prayers with his teaching about forgiveness'. This suggestion seems to be confirmed by the number of words in Matthew's version which are characteristic of Matthew himself: *Father in heaven; kingdom come; earth/heaven; today; debts* as a synonym for sins; *the evil one*. The rather surprising phrase, 'bread for the coming day', might be suggested by the story of the Israelites being fed each day with manna for the day ahead. In this way we should have an explanation for the absence of the Prayer in Mark and its presence in Matthew. Jesus did not teach the Prayer as it stands, but it really is his teaching about prayer, partly direct but principally by his example in Gethsemane: our familiar form is therefore the creation of Matthew.

If Austin Farrer was right, and Luke had a copy of Matthew's Gospel, then we should have an explanation for the Lucan version also. For just as Matthew's version has a considerable number of expressions characteristic of Matthew, so Luke's form of the Prayer has a number of expressions typical of Luke: *Father,* (comma)*; each day; forgive sins.* Luke often abbreviates the earlier Gospels, and he might easily find Matthew rather fulsome with his theme 'We are on earth, but thou art in heaven'. This explanation seems to be confirmed by Luke's curious use of the word *indebted*; this word fitted well with Matthew's *debts,* but it doesn't fit after Luke's *sins.* It looks as if Luke has simply carried the word over from Matthew's version by oversight.

The argument seemed powerful, and I was pleased but not surprised when it was accepted by Hedley Sparks for the *JTS,* in which it was published under the title 'The Composition of the Lord's Prayer'. This success was important for me in several ways. First, with two articles over my name in the foremost Journal, I was establishing myself as a recognized scholar. But also I was helping to set up two theories of which I was to be a long-time advocate. Before this it had been normal to say that Luke's version was the older form, preserved in Q, a lost source, and that Matthew's version was a later expansion by Matthew. I was now suggesting that Matthew, and to some degree Luke also, felt themselves free to adapt and amplify traditional words of Jesus; this creativity was an important new idea, not quickly welcomed. At the same time I was providing evidence that Austin was right: the hypothetical source Q was a mare's nest; the simpler explanation was correct, that Luke had a copy of Matthew's as well as of Mark's Gospel. This met with even hotter resistance.

After the success of the Dinner, I put my hand to two or three further initiatives, which met with less success. In the summer of 1958 there was organized a Billy Graham Crusade in Manchester. The news was greeted with general hostility in the Press: it was theologically naïve, it was musically substandard ('a majestic hymn by Haydn and two dreadful caterwaulings by Anon'—*The Guardian),* it was emotional, it was American. I found some of these rather snobbish objections echoed by some of my clerical colleagues; but I felt that Graham had a long history of successful preaching, both in America and in London,

and that I should give him the benefit of the doubt and support the
endeavour. The sponsors were experienced, and the Crusade was well
organized. Being held in Manchester, it was within a hundred miles
of half the people in the country, and coach-loads attended from West
Yorkshire, Lancashire, and the Midlands. The Crusade was in two parts.
The first was a preaching of the evangelical gospel by an unappealing
man called Dan Pyatt; this was intended for established members of the
churches, who were to become 'counsellors' at Graham's own sermons.
I encouraged a good party of our church members to attend this course,
and I urged the Youth Club to come and hear Billy himself. The meetings
were moving, sheerly through the huge number of people attending, and
the singing of what had now become favourites, like 'O Lord my God...
How great Thou art'. Billy turned out to be a humble and attractive
man, with a straightforward and simple message, which he put over
with considerable force. At the end of his address he appealed to those
present to come forward and 'give themselves to Christ'; those who did
this were allocated to counsellors, who spoke with them briefly, took
their names and local churches, which were later informed so that they
could follow up the converts. I was a little embarrassed by the presence
of my brother Terence, who was staying with us at the time and who
came along to see what it was like. Such an appeal was unnatural to him,
and his detachment made me feel that I was advocating something he
would regard as phoney. A number of our young people did go up and
became, at least for a while, keener churchgoers; but I felt dissatisfied
with the overall experience and would not wish to do the same thing
again.

Among the Church's more successful enterprises at this time was
Lee Abbey, a holiday centre in Devonshire; this was attended by large
numbers of young people from (mostly evangelical) churches across
the country. Its attraction was a combination of Outward Bound-type
activities, and well-led spiritual exercises. While on holiday in the area
myself I called in and was impressed by the place. The Director, Canon
Geoffrey Paul, was an able man who could give addresses and Bible
studies which the holiday-makers enjoyed; and his staff led groups on
walks, climbs, etc. The place was humming and obviously very popular.
I was interested therefore to hear that a parallel centre was to be opened
in North Lancashire at a place called Scargill. I thought that this might
be a useful experience for our own people, and when I suggested it, the
idea was taken up by about a dozen older church members. I arranged
a weekend with the new Director, Mr Barker, and we set off in cars on
a cold winter's afternoon. When we reached the area, snow was falling,

the hills were steep, and the driving not easy; but we pressed on and arrived safely. Barker and his vice-Director, Dick Marsh, gave us a warm welcome, but sadly we were the only party attending as the other churches had been put off by the bad weather. The weather cleared up the next day and we were sent out on various athletic exercises. Dick was a mountaineer, who had climbed K2 in the Himalayas, and he encouraged us to attempt climbing a rock face. To my chagrin I lost my nerve while eighteen inches (I mean inches) off the ground and dared move neither up nor down. Despite this failure I enjoyed the visit; our talks with the Directors were encouraging, and I felt that there was an opening for parties from the parish to come there and be much edified. Sadly nothing came of this hopeful beginning: a few weeks after our visit Dick was climbing the rock face partly supported by new nylon ropes, but one of these frayed and he fell to the ground and was killed. Such an accident to a leader was a deterrent to more ordinary people. Scargill continued for years, but we never sent another party to it in my time.

I made many mistakes while I was at St Christopher's, but one of them was serious. One of the first supermarkets had opened in Withington, and when I called on my parishioners, they would often ask me whether I thought they should continue to support their local shops, or was it all right to go for the cheaper prices at the supermarket? I thought, unwarily, that I should devote the Rector's Letter in the Parish Magazine to an even-handed discussion of this matter. The local shops had served the people faithfully for years, and needed the business if they were to stay open; service there was friendly and personal, and sometimes included credit, and house-delivery. On the other hand, some families were stretched for money, and needed to take advantage of lower prices where they were available. The article brought down a storm of anger on my head. I had not imagined the seriousness of the threat which these supermarkets represented to the livelihood of the small shopkeepers. They were faced with ruin, and could see it more clearly than I. Also, one or two of the shops advertised in the magazine, and not unreasonably felt that I might have supported them without qualification. My wife was shocked and upset when Mr Tudor refused to serve her, and she was compelled to walk a mile, pushing the pram, to get a loaf of bread or a piece of fish.

It was not only local shopkeepers with whom I had to deal; the issue was taken up in the Press, and I was asked to discuss the matter on local radio. This led to a most distressing episode. I had an invitation from a shopkeeper in Walkden (pron. Wogden) to come and visit his home. Clare and I went there by bus, and as we approached we passed an enormous new Tesco's, with full lights blazing, long after closing-time. The shopkeeper's situation was indeed grim. He showed me a cup and saucer which he was offering as a gift to any customer who would spend money at his shop, a pathetic contrast to the arrogant self-advertisement of the supermarket. His house was damp, so much so that the pyjamas of his three boys had to be draped over a clothes-horse to be aired by the fire before they could put them on at night. The boys had all won places at Manchester Grammar School, but he was having difficulty finding money for the fees and uniform. We saw their pale faces as they laboured away at their homework, and felt that they deserved better than this. I felt bitterly ashamed to have been so out of touch with the real situation of such people; one ought to get to know the background, and possible consequences, before giving opinions, and it is not sensible to speak of an 'even-handed' discussion when the issue is between humble people facing ruin and well-capitalized companies seeking market dominance.

My last years at St Christopher's were gladdened by the arrival of a curate, Brian Morgan, who came with his wife Edythe, and soon they became good friends to us. I was supposedly training Brian, but in fact I learned much more from him than I taught him. His father was a butcher, and she came from Rochdale, and their background made them far more in touch with the parishioners than I was. We had no television set, but the Morgans had one, and liked to watch 'Coronation Street' and 'Match of the Day', and so could relate quite naturally to the parishioners in a way I never could. They were both sterling characters, and were to give lives of devoted service to the Church—in Trinidad, Lourenco Marques, and Rotterdam, where Brian was Missions to Seamen Chaplain, and later in several parishes in Lancashire. At a time when I was rather isolated in the parish, it was marvellous to have the support of such a couple; and I was delighted when they asked me to be godfather to their adopted son Paul.

My last months at St Christopher's were marred by the souring of relations with the Beagles family. I mentioned above that Beagles had been the keenest one to urge my predecessor to leave the parish, and he wanted a dominant voice in the conduct of church affairs. When I disagreed with him he could turn unpleasant, telling me on a number of occasions that I was 'pig-'eaded'. He fell ill with cancer about a year after my arrival, and I visited him faithfully each evening and took him Communion. He appreciated this, but we were always oppressed by the presence of his family, who lived next door to us. Mrs Beagles used to take the licence of walking into the Rectory by the back door uninvited, and shouting 'Coo-ee!', which infuriated Clare. Beagles had been a

Local Government employee, and wangled himself the four-bedroom house next to the Rectory, from which he could keep an eye on all that happened. At the end of each year the church had an Annual General Meeting, at which comments were welcome on church affairs In 1962, to my dismay, Beagles rose to say, 'We have been keeping an eye on you, Rector. When first you came you used to go out visiting at half past two in the afternoon. Nowadays you often don't go out till half past three'. I had never dreamed that I would be publicly accused of idleness, after so much hard work; and the afternoon hour was not spent at leisure, but in preparing work for publication—though this would not have been a justification in the eyes of Beagles, who said I was not paid to do this.

The work on which I had been engaged was an extension of the theme advanced in my article on Luke 1–2 and Genesis. This had opened my eyes to the possibility that other parts of the New Testament were composed in the same way. It seemed, for example, that Luke had written the Acts of the Apostles not just to give an account of the early Church, but also to present the story as a repeat of the pattern of the life of Jesus. In Acts 27, for example, Paul's ship is driven by the storm for fourteen days, and he then presides at a final meal in which he blesses bread, breaks it, and shares it round those present. This raises a strong echo of the Last Supper where Jesus presides and similarly breaks and distributes bread, on Passover night, that is, the fourteenth night of Nisan. There is a believable echo following in that Paul is providentially delivered from death by drowning as the ship hits a shoal off the Maltese beach; the Christian reader may well reflect on the similarity to the story of Jesus's resurrection. I combined all the apparent parallels of this kind in a volume which I entitled *Type and History in Acts*.

The 'type' here is the pattern of Jesus's life which underlies the story of the history of the Church. Not all the references were equally cogent, and when the book was published in 1964 reviewers gave it the Bronx cheer; but the general theme remains impressive, and led on to my later conclusion that Luke was, in both his Gospel and in the Acts, a creative writer.

Beagles' remarks at the parish AGM had been made worse by some bitter comments by his daughter Barbara, and I began to think it was time for me to go; and as it happened an opportunity presented itself at just this point. Back in December 1958 I had had a surprising letter from Bishop Hall in Hong Kong: he was intending to retire in 1963, and thought that I would be a very suitable person to succeed him; I was to discuss this with Clare and let him know how we thought, but we were enjoined not to mention the matter to our families or anyone else. This was certainly a bolt from the blue: to me R.O. was a saint, and the thought of succeeding him in his life's work made me feel totally unworthy. The truth was that he erred on the side of sentimentalising; not only I, but all his geese were swans; he had had few ordinands with degrees from Cambridge or such universities, and he knew me to be a sincere and hardworking priest, with plenty of sympathy for ordinary Chinese people. Clare and I discussed the proposal; she felt reluctant to go so far, and for an open-ended commitment, but she was willing to give it a try. I felt that it was work I might be happy doing, and for all my limitations I had the intellectual gifts and the pastoral commitment to make something of it. Meanwhile, I carried on with my work at St Christopher's. But, nearly three years later, at about the time of the parish AGM in 1962, I received a more specific proposal from the Bishop. Candidates for the priesthood in the diocese of Hong Kong were trained at a small college, the Union Theological College (UTC), sited in Hong Kong University; the Principal was about to retire, and the Bishop thought it would be a good idea for me to come out and take his place. This would give me a chance 'to see and to be seen' before the election of the next Bishop. It was not of course in R.O.'s power to nominate his successor, and the new Bishop had to be elected by two houses, one Chinese, one English; if I had been active in the diocese for some months people would (he thought) have had a chance to recognize my suitability. At the moment there were nine students in the UTC, all graduates, but under my leadership the number would grow, and there would be several other teachers to assist me.

This invitation came therefore at a timely moment for me. But I was hesitant about accepting so heavy a responsibility, partly from awareness of my general failings, and partly from uncertainty about the basis of my Christian faith. This second anxiety was exacerbated by the fact that Clare's faith, which had been so strong in Oxford days, had ebbed under pressure of parochial disappointment. I decided to take counsel with Bishop Greer, a kindly if somewhat Olympian figure, two metres high. He was quietly reassuring: he was less concerned over his own inadequacies than over those of his clergy; Hong Kong was a small diocese, and I should do little harm. This was not the encouragement I was looking for, but we decided nonetheless to accept the offer, even though Clare felt that it might become a sentence for life. We were to sail in August, but judged it prudent to postpone the announcement of our departure till July. But back in March Nicholas, our five-year-old, had written in his 'news' at school that we were going to Hong Kong; his faithful teacher, suspecting correctly that this was not for publication, kept it to herself, and only told us when we said goodbye to her in July.

Chapter 9

HONG KONG

We arrived in Hong Kong on 30th September, 1962, and my introduction
to the UTC was a disappointment: just as R.O.'s opinion of me had
been mostly wishful thinking, so had been his account of the College.
There were indeed nine students, but only six of them, the Anglicans,
were full-time, the remainder being mere visitors from other churches.
They were by no means all graduates in the normal sense of the word;
R.O. introduced the first of them to me, 'This is Peter Pau, a graduate
from the University of Life'—this meant that his formal education had
ceased when he left school at thirteen. Only Benjamin Pau was a proper
graduate; Chang Kwok-Wai had so little English that he could not follow
the lectures and needed coaching by Clare. So far from the college
growing under my leadership, the number of Anglican students had to
be limited, as the Church could only support three ordinations a year.
Nor was the assistant staff impressive. I had a full-time number two, a
friendly American called Tad Evans; he was keen to teach theology, which
suited me in my hesitant mood, but he was soon to be transferred to be a
chaplain in the US Army in Vietnam. The Revd Luke Cheung, a Chinese
vicar, came in to teach the New Testament. I walked in by mistake on
one of his lectures, and found him dictating from the notes which he had
made as a student in the Church Divinity School of the Pacific. I could
not help wondering whether these in turn had been dictated from the
CDSP tutor's own days in college, and so on back to St Peter. The Old
Testament was taught by the saintly but sentimental Canon Martin. At
my first examiners' meeting he told us that the UTC had a high standard,
and that the pass mark was therefore sixty percent; but when he found
that he had given fewer than sixty marks to each of the students, he
'realized that he had been unjust' and made up the difference. The only
genuine scholar was the gentle but invalid Lei Shiu-Keung; he taught
Church History, and had read Justin in an English translation, happily
drawing parallels with Chinese links between religion and philosophy.
A visiting Methodist came in and taught 'Comparative Religion', in fact
a dreary account of various non-Christian faiths. In this situation, I felt

I had to plug the gaps: I taught courses in Ethics, Homiletics, subjects which I had never studied, and a new course in Marxism, which seemed to me a more important thing for the students to know about, though here again my knowledge had to be assimilated quickly from what I could read. Also in time I gave Luke Cheung the sack, so as to enable me to teach the students something I knew about.

As these facts sank in, I could hardly avoid the conclusion that my job description had been thoroughly misleading. Fortunately, since R.O. was my hero, I was not disposed to accuse him of dishonesty; but his invitation had been coloured by his wish to see me in place for his successor's election. Even the title of the college, Union Theological College, was misleading. The name had been that of a predecessor in Canton before the war; but that had been a union of Anglican, Methodist, and Presbyterian candidates for the ministry, while my UTC was effectively for Anglicans only. It did not take me long to realize that the basic flaw in its structure was that it was too small: there were not enough students for them to learn from each other, and the staff were insufficiently learned or varied. I soon set about enquiring after other colleges in the Colony. I could not collaborate with any Catholic institution, partly from my dislike of Catholic dogma, but also because Catholics despised Anglicans. But I found three friendly Protestant colleges, with whom I quickly made good relations. The Methodists and Presbyterians now had their own institution at Chung Chi in the New Territories. There was a considerable Lutheran college, run by Americans from Missouri; this latter point was a pity as Missouri Lutherans are mostly rigid fundamentalists. But I especially liked the staff at the Basel Mission college; their Old Testament teacher, Richard Deutsch, could read the Hebrew Bible in the original, and the Principal, Nathanael Wieder, was an impressive man. He had a sense of humour, though his English was limited; later, when Bishop Robinson's *Honest to God* caused a scandal, I invited him to review the book to an audience of clergy and teachers. I introduced him as 'Dr Wieder', to which he replied, 'Permit me to demythologize myself: I am not a doctor'. His critique was good, but unfortunately he referred to the book throughout as 'Faithful to God', which was not quite what Robinson intended. I hoped that it might be possible for these three colleges in some way to pool their resources with the UTC, but R.O. did not like the idea and it may have been impracticable. It was four years before he allowed the notion to be discussed by the Chinese canons, who were the Board governing the UTC. But then Canon Chung said, 'We must maintain our Anglican standards', and that was the end of the idea. I resigned at that point; I could not go on serving an institution which I knew to be unviable.

Meanwhile, I found myself drawn into taking some part in public affairs. Soon after my arrival, the Hong Kong Government made a surprising announcement: any civil servant who wished to send his child to an English public school would have half the cost paid by the Government. This was in effect a sizable bonus for the already well-paid expatriate, in a situation where there was no free education for the ordinary Chinese child. This seemed scandalous to me, and I said so to Geoffrey Speak, the Headmaster of St Paul's, the prestigious Anglican Boys' school. He fully agreed, but told me that as a teacher in a Government-subsidized school he was forbidden publicly to criticize Government policy. I said to him that if he would give me the bullets, I would fire them. At the time Hong Kong was ruled by a Governor, Sir David Trench, who was advised by a Legislative Council, half of whose members were civil servants, and half millionaires; the most effective means of protest was therefore the Press, and the South China Morning Post ran a daily correspondence column. So I took advantage of information passed to me by Geoffrey and wrote a piece of English prose, which was published, and was surprisingly effective. The civil servants belonged to a union, with officers in England, and they sent for a spokesman to fly out to the Colony and debate with me on Radio Hong Kong. I viewed his arrival with nervousness, for he would be an experienced professional negotiator, and I had no experience in this field. But in the event I won the day handsomely: I was well-informed, the Government's action was in fact scandalous, and I was quick on my feet and articulate. I could tell that it had gone well by the fact that when Clare and I were asked out to dinner, other guests working for the Government were cold and rude to me. I was well satisfied with the incident at the time; I had given an example to the UTC students that it was suitable to take a public stand on an issue of justice, and it was no harm for the community to feel that the Church had taken a lead on such an issue. In the longer term things were not quite so good. It was six months before the Bishop persuaded Trench to receive a deputation on the matter. This consisted of two clergy, Robin Howard, Vicar of Christ Church, Kowloon Tong, and me, and two head teachers, one of whom was Geoffrey Speak. Trench adroitly divided us: the head teachers were dependent on Government goodwill for the treatment of their schools, and it would be disastrous if he realized that Geoffrey had fed me information. So neither he nor the other head spoke firmly, and the Governor was able to speak to us dismissively as a couple of amateur trouble-makers. I felt betrayed.

A happy side-effect of this incident was my making friends with Pat Penn, an intelligent woman who was in charge of religious broadcasting for Radio Hong Kong. She encouraged me to submit a regular feature, and I took up the challenge. I remembered a BBC programme before the War, in which the anchor-man told a story involving a moral dilemma, and ended, 'What would you do, chum?' I adopted the same format without the formula: I called the series 'The Spur of the Moment', and was able to find enough stories with moral problems to keep it running for eight or nine weeks. Pat regarded me as a resource to comment on religious issues, and this produced one uncomfortable interlude. For some reason she wanted a comment on the Ecumenical Movement, and asked Robin Howard and me to say something about it. There was not much doubt about the facts: there had been a large Church conference at Edinburgh in 1910, and a Free Churchman, J.H. Oldham, pointed out the scandal of different churches sending missionaries to the same country, who then competed for converts. He proposed that the Protestant churches join together in a world-wide movement, for which he chose the word ecumenical from the Greek *oecumene*, the world. This was taken up and the churches cooperated quite effectively, forming the World Council of Churches, and other similar bodies. Robin and I were in full agreement about this; what we hadn't expected was that our piece was followed by one by a Catholic priest, Father Collins. Collins gave a most annoying talk: the real beginning of the movement, he said, was about forty years earlier, when a Catholic nun had received a vision calling her to begin a world-wide movement to bring all churches together in obedience to the Pope. Robin and I were furious: we were both persuaded that the nun and her vision were fictitious, and that Collins was totally distorting the history in order to make it seem that the movement was one to bring obedience to Rome. There was, however, nothing we could do but sit and fume; we were given no opportunity to respond, and if we had been my comments would have been unprintable. My sole resource was a brief Parthian shot: Collins finished his talk by saying, 'The Catholic speaker next week will be Father Barbieri, from...' he was going to add, '...from the Pontifical Institute at Rome', or some other prestigious institution, but in the heat of the moment he forgot which. I was in time to supply the gap, 'from Siviglia'.

My busyness in the public arena did not prevent me from using my imagination for a programme for the UTC. Hong Kong was an island ceded by China in 1841, with an extensive hinterland, the New Territories, leased for a century in 1897. These territories included a number of islands separated by normally smooth waters, which were suitable for canoeing. I thought the students would enjoy an expedition, in canoes which I hired, and we set forth together, spending the night in a church hall in the country, where we were able to make a warm meal. The enterprise was successful; like many physical exercises it had the effect of binding us together, and I was grateful to the others for some help, when my weak left arm made it difficult for me to keep the paddling up. We said Compline together in the late evening, and returned safely home next day. Less successful was another, later exercise. I used to invite visiting speakers to an informal meeting of the College on Friday evenings, and one of these was the Bishop's industrial chaplain, a Eurasian called Denham Crary. Denham was rather contemptuous of the study programme at the College, which he thought would cut no ice with the ordinary Hong Kong worker. He thought a good preparation for a pastoral ministry among workers would be for the students to take a job as workers during the holiday period. I thought it was difficult to deny this, and the students were willing, though in some cases reluctant. In the result the jobs we undertook proved mostly too tough for us. I felt I should take part myself, and engaged to decorate the parish hall of one of the churches. Again my weak left arm proved a serious handicap and I was relieved when I came to the end of the fortnight. The others got jobs which were often quite unsuitable, such as working in a tannery, where the fumes were so unpleasant as to make them sick. It may be that Denham was right, and that more was learned, even if unpleasantly learned, in this 'holiday' than in all the term-time; but the experience was not enjoyed and did a good deal to lower student morale.

The UTC was housed in St John's College, a fine eight-storey block high on the hillside in the University area. The two top storeys were given to girl students; the four storeys below for male students, with my UTC students among them; there were public rooms on the ground floor, and we ourselves had a large flat on the second floor, with a spacious verandah overlooking the harbour. In return for this I was 'Senior Tutor' to the students, and responsible for discipline. In general this was not troublesome; but in the first week of each year I was embroiled in a battle to stop the 'initiation' of the new students by their predecessors. This had been introduced, ultimately from America and consisted in the 'hazing', that is the bullying of the greenhorns, sometimes physical, sometimes psychological or financial—e.g. they were made to pay for a restaurant dinner for their whole floor, but prevented from joining in the eating themselves. I was furious to find nervous young students waiting their turn to be hectored and tormented; I determined to stop this cruel practice, and forbade it on threat of expulsion from the college. Such a sadistic tradition was not easily to be broken, and when I was defied, I took the promised action and dismissed the main miscreant. This caused an uproar; his friends petitioned to have him reinstated, and appealed over my head to the Fellows of the college. These academics rarely met, but I was delighted that they fully supported me and confirmed my decision. I had at least the satisfaction that the same trouble did not recur the following year.

Life in the college was not all plain sailing. In our second year there was a severe drought, and drinking water was limited to four hours' supply every fourth day. But the college lavatory system depended on water piped in from a hillside stream; and this stream also supplied water for farmers growing lettuces further down the hill. During this time these farmers would climb up and stuff leaves and other detritus into the mouth of our pipe, and I had to go with the college *fa-wong* (gardener) to unstuff the pipe. We also had a typhoon one night which demolished the servants' quarters, and, clinging onto trees, we helped the students to salvage their bedding and possessions as they flew into the air, and transferred them to the safety of the main building.

While Tad Evans was with us, theology was a live topic at the UTC: Tad had read John Robinson's *Honest to God,* and thought it was the best thing out. But reviews told me that the book was highly controversial in England, and I could not easily concur with his enthusiasm. Robinson had a powerful journalistic style, as when he denied the existence of a 'God out there', and I could fully sympathize with his despair over personal prayer; but the positive content was unclear to me, and this became an acute difficulty, as person after person asked me over the next two years and beyond, what I thought of the book. Alastair MacIntyre, a respected philosopher, said that not only was Robinson an atheist, but so also were Tillich and other celebrated German theologians on whom he depended. I did not want to call Robinson an atheist myself, but I did not feel clear enough about his gospel of 'panentheism' to commend it. The controversy in fact merely added to my own theological uncomfortableness.

When Tad left for Vietnam, he was replaced by a delightful, relaxed, fat clergyman called John Yates, somewhat larger than life, who became a close friend, and whose geniality was a helpful antidote to my own rather over-zealous approach. John was part-time my deputy, and part-time chaplain at the Cathedral. His laid-back approach infuriated the serious Dean, John Foster: John would say he had spent four hours visiting parishioners, when in fact he had been playing Bridge, what he called 'visiting in depth'; this was not just an excuse, he claimed, but doing this would make for a deeper relationship than if he simply visited from house to house. He was a *bon viveur*; he enjoyed good meals at restaurants, he entertained my children to expensive teas at the Hong Kong Hilton, and invited the students on his floor in the College to a 'snake party', a Chinese delicacy. He much enjoyed books, and his sermons were often delightful; in time he became the enthusiastic, and successful, manager of the church's Challenge Bookshop. I gave him a copy of my *Type and History in Acts*, when it came out, on which he made the helpful comment that I would never be a real scholar until I could read Hebrew and German. This was a warning to which I later gave heed. John's weakness was his liability to fall in love with unsuitable girls, often Roman Catholics. He would say, 'Girls in headscarves knock me sideways'. Sadly this was in the end his undoing: returned to England, he married too quickly a woman who did not much care for him, and when she left him he took refuge in the bottle, and died, unhappily, in his forties.

About this time R.O. asked me to go as representative of the diocese to the Philippines. These islands had been colonized by the Spaniards since the sixteenth century, and the people on the plains had been converted to Catholicism; but the missionaries had carefully left the head-hunting tribes alone in the mountains. When the USA took the Spanish empire over in the 1890s, the Episcopal (Anglican) Church took over responsibility for these mountain peoples, called the Igorot. These people continued a very simple life: the women did all the work, both in the field and in the home; the men had the duty of defending the village. Each morning a posse of them would go armed with spears to patrol the village boundaries, and make sure there had been no incursions by hostile neighbours. There had in fact been no such incursions for seventy years, but one cannot be too safe. Education seemed the most promising way forward for such people. Churches had been founded among them, but no schools, and the Bishop there had asked R.O. to send someone familiar with the Anglican investment in Hong Kong schools, which was very large, to report on our experience in education. I flew to Manila, and made good relations with the Canon appointed to meet me, and I was then taken up into the hills above the town of Baguio. Here I met the American vicar, who told me they were to found a school the next day, and there would be a 'dog-party' to celebrate this. I was asked to make a speech, and then, the vicar, in some confusion, said, 'Will you say Grace, Mr Hong Kong?'. To my dismay, I realized that I was asking Divine blessing on the eating of a dog—a traditional festal dish in the Philippines. Despite my revulsion I could not offend my hosts, so I ate what I was given.

Back in Manila, I was invited to visit the Theological College. This was much better staffed than the UTC, but the discipline seemed to be imposed on the students rather than agreed, and I preferred the atmosphere at my own institution. Most noticeable among the teachers was an enormously fat priest in a cassock, who smoked like a chimney; this was Father Chandlee, an American who taught liturgy, a High Church ecclesiastic, typically self-indulgent, who was interested in the flummery of church services rather than the religion behind them. A couple of months later Chandlee came on a visit to Hong Kong, and it was natural for me to be asked to entertain him. Our daughters were much struck by his chain-smoking and laboured breathing, and christened him 'Puffy Wheeze-Bag'. This was not to be the last time our paths crossed.

I was the obvious host for distinguished visitors, some more congenial than others. On the boat going on leave, R.O. had read *We Teach Them Wrong*, by Sir Richard Acland, a specialist in religious education. The book was an attack on excessive emphasis on biblical authority, and R.O. feared that there was the same tendency in his own church schools. He wrote to invite Acland to come and give lectures to the Hong Kong teachers. This invitation he accepted; but before he became interested in R.E., Sir Richard had been an MP with extreme left-wing views. He was in fact more interested in the Chinese revolution than in the Hong Kong schools, and immediately on arrival he took a week off to visit China and see the marvels of Mao's Great Leap Forward. When he finally returned to the colony, he was a great embarrassment: if China was a workers' paradise, Hong Kong was a pattern instance of capitalism grinding the faces of the poor. He went out with his camera to find evidence of this truth, and returned triumphant after a morning's stroll. He had seen a building site, and on it a worker pushing a wheelbarrow at the double. He did not have the Cantonese to interview the man, but the scene spoke for itself, and he never ceased from repeating this incident while he was with us. I had to chair his lectures when he came to give them, and they were a worse embarrassment. He was a copybook example of a bad teacher. The content of the lectures was neither clear nor interesting, and the delivery spoiled by quirks of behaviour: he distracted his audience by incessantly hoisting up his trousers; he referred frequently to the theologian Paul Tillich, but mispronounced the last syllable as 'itch', which caused some English teachers, impatient with his performance, to barrack him by repeating the 'tch' every time he so pronounced it. I was powerless to stop this rudeness, and thought I would only make things worse if I intervened.

Tillich's name was much in the air at the time, thanks to *Honest to God*, and the subsequent paperback theology; and I thought there might well be a take-up for a society providing for a discussion of the issues raised. I launched a William Temple Society, and there was indeed a good response. Some forty people came for the evening once a month to our flat, and the principal difficulty was to find a panel of adequate speakers. As it turned out there was enough talent, and the standard was quite high. The most memorable paper was by Philip Shen, who taught Theology in the Chinese University. His title was '*The Theology of My Fair Lady*', and he offered an interesting discussion of the difference between the endings in Shaw's play *Pygmalion* and its musical version.

I did so much of the teaching at the UTC that I was always on the lookout for anyone who could give the students more variety; and I was pleased to find that a C.M.S missionary, Joyce Bennett, had done some postgraduate study in New Testament. R.O. had persuaded her to become Headmistress of a Chinese-language Middle School for girls, St Catherine's, Kwun Tong; but she was willing to come and give a lecture once a week for us. Her lectures were enjoyed, and she used to come down to my flat in St John's College afterwards for a cup of coffee and a chat. She told me that she thought there was a good number of teachers and other such people who would like a better knowledge of the Bible; and suggested that we might together teach a course in her flat once a week in the evening. This was to lead to an exam and a qualification, the Diocesan Diploma in Theology, or D.D.T., its initials coinciding with those of a then popular pesticide. The initiative was well taken up; about twenty-five people gathered in Joyce's flat on Tuesday evenings, some sitting on the floor. She gave a lecture on the Old Testament, and I one on the New, with an interval between for tea and relaxation. Those attending were mostly Chinese teachers in secondary schools, wives of clergy, and Sunday School superintendents.

At the time we were congratulating ourselves on the success of our initiative, the UTC Board met and declined my suggestion of a wider partnership between ourselves and other theological colleges. I felt that the present set-up was not in the students' best interest, and I resigned as Principal, in the hope that their education might be organized on a better basis. A successor was appointed, but soon afterwards the UTC fused with the Chung Chi College, which was not much different from what I had intended.

Joyce asked me what I thought I might do next. I wished I could answer this question. I did not want to go back to parish ministry, now that my faith seemed so insecure; but I didn't know what else would be open to me. A few days later she rang to say she had seen an advertisement in an avant-garde Christian journal, *Prism*, for a Tutor in Theology in the Extramural Department of the University of Birmingham, a post which sounded similar to the work we had been doing together. This sounded interesting, but the next call came to say that sadly the journal had been thrown away. However, a day or so later her amah managed to rescue it from the lap-sap. By such a slender thread did my whole future come to hang. The details, when they came, were discouraging: the date for applications was already past, and it had taken three weeks for the paper to come out from England. Nonetheless I thought I would apply. There was no time to write round for references, so I wrote my own, without too much modesty—'I have had three articles published in J.T.S, and a book on the Acts; I read Latin and Greek, and speak French, German, Italian, and Cantonese. I have taught courses for adults both lay and clergy, English and Chinese'. This involved some elasticity of language as I could not converse for long in either German or Cantonese, but the latter weakness was not likely to be discovered. To my surprise and pleasure I received a response by return, asking if I could come for interview in May. I had to tell them that we were not sailing from Hong Kong until 3 June, and would not be back in England until early July. They duly interviewed all the other candidates, but held the post open till they could see me; and so I thought I stood a good chance of getting it.

Meanwhile R.O. had announced his own retirement, and the election of his successor had to be undertaken. By a church canon this task was entrusted to two houses, one Chinese- and one English-speaking. My name was proposed, but clearly had little support among the English electors, partly no doubt following my involvement in political issues. More important, a famous man was suggested, Joost de Blank, a South African liberal who had become Bishop of Stepney. Once he accepted the invitation, there was absolutely no prospect of my succeeding R.O., a cause for much relief to me. As things fell out, Joost de Blank had a heart attack and was forced to withdraw, and the next Bishop was in fact the amiable Gilbert Baker, whom I have referred to above. So I was free to set sail with my family for England; we said goodbye to many friends, but with most regret to our amah Ah Kwan, and our dog Paddington, and on 3 June 1966 we sailed for home on the Italian liner *Asia*. Clare, who had been so reluctant to come to Hong Kong, was now equally sad to be leaving; she had found a good use for her time there in teaching Chinese boys at St Paul's College, which she had much enjoyed.

Chapter 10

ALL SAINTS, KINGS HEATH

We reached England early in July, and the interview for the University job, so long held over, was to take place a few days later. I set forth from my in-laws' home near Chester in good time, but in my haste had left behind me the map which had been kindly supplied. This resulted in a certain amount of panic as I drove round the University area vainly looking for my Department. Luckily I stopped to enquire at a bus-stop and a man offered to accompany me to the building I was looking for. I arrived about three minutes late, but had calmed down by the time the interview began. It was chaired by Prof. Gordon Davies, the Head of the Theology Department. He had looked at my *JTS* articles, and asked me a series of questions about these and related subjects. I knew my texts well and was able to defend what I had written, so I could speak with confidence and directness. After about twenty minutes I began to relax, feeling that the interview was going quite well. But Davies then handed proceedings over to Prof. Smart, the second Professor in his Department. Smart gave me a friendly smile, and bowled me what looked like a half-volley: 'If we gave you the job, Mr Goulder, would you arrange any courses in religions other than Christianity?' The question seemed easy, but I did not find it so. I have always thought that pussy-footing does you no good: if you say, 'Oh yes, I am very keen on that', you are bound to be asked supplementary questions which will reveal your insincerity. My mind went back to the soporific hour in which I had heard a Methodist visitor teaching the UTC students about Buddhism; and I thought, 'Better to be forthright and at least be seen to be honest', so I said boldly, 'To tell you the truth, I think it is the most boring subject out!' In one way this reply could hardly have been more successful: the room was filled immediately with loud guffaws of laughter. Smart was well known (though not by me) as the national proponent of teaching non-Christian religions in Theology Departments. He explained that there were large numbers of Hindus, Muslims, and Sikhs in the Midlands, and people might be interested to understand their beliefs. I don't know whether my rash words did me good or harm, but the important thing was that I was offered the job.

Having secured this, I went on to find a house to live in, which Clare and I succeeded in doing almost immediately. It was a six-bedroom house in Kings Heath, built in 1899, with a large garden. We were able to move in on 11 September 1966, which was a Sunday. I drove the family up from my mother's in Surrey, and as we came through King's Heath we noticed a fine Victorian church, All Saints, at the crossroads. The people who had sold us our house had warned us against this church, as it was old-fashioned; but we had not been to church that day, and it was getting late, so we decided to ignore their advice and give it a try, without revealing that I was a clergyman. We were seated at the back of the church, and all went well until a spherical figure rolled down the aisle and led the prayers in an American accent. Loud stage whispers from our sharp-eyed daughters informed us that this was none other than 'Puffy Wheezebag', Father Chandlee from Manila. Our cover was inevitably blown, and to our dismay we were introduced to the welcoming clergy. Father May, the Vicar, was a moderate Anglo-Catholic, a tall, dignified figure with the authority of a prophet. He had no incense or confessions, but there was a marked sympathy for the Church of Rome. He was a kindly and good man, and soon invited me to be an auxiliary member of the staff, celebrating Communion and preaching, despite my appalling singing voice and occasional lapses into referring to the C. of E. as Protestant. He is also remembered for presiding at parish cricket matches, where his favourite shot, a lofted straight drive high over the bowler's head, came to be known as 'a Father May'. He had a delightful curate, Rodney Whiteman, and I soon became part of a happy fellowship.

This continued for some time, in fact until Father May retired and Rodney left to take up a parish of his own. The new Vicar was Michael Walls, a liberal white South African. The appointment was probably a mistake. Michael had been an industrial chaplain, and was more at home with working men than with the staid middle-class congregation at All Saints. Also he and his wife were deeply interested in the Indian communities in the Midlands. Su (without an 'e') was a teacher in a poor school in an immigrant district, and spent her Saturday afternoons refereeing hockey matches between teams of children of Indian and Pakistani extraction. The vicarage lawn was often an encampment for children from her school invited for the day. All this meant that Michael never really settled in, and after two years he decided to leave All Saints, and took up a temporary post teaching French in a school. This move resulted in a certain crisis. Michael's successor was announced, and the wardens wanted to decorate the vicarage before he arrived. There was plenty of time, but the wardens had taken Michael's premature resignation as a slight to the church, and asked him to be out of the house just two days before his own house could be ready to receive him. Michael asked if he could delay the move by these two days, but was told that he could always move his furniture into store, a thing he and Su could ill afford. This brought me into the picture. I was acting as locum during the interregnum, and was due to preach on the following Sunday evening. I went to see the wardens, to intercede for Michael, but was met with a blank refusal. I looked up the lessons for the service when I would be preaching, and in the second lesson it is laid down that one should make up a quarrel, first by seeing one's opponent privately, and then, if he will not listen, to 'tell it to the church'. This looked to me like the inspiration for what I should say, and I went to the church with my sermon in my hand, fully armed. To my surprise I was greeted at the door by the warden with a letter telling me that they had decided to allow Michael the extra two days. I told him what I had been going to say, and he was much relieved to be spared the embarrassment. He did however leave me with the problem of what theme I should preach on instead. Fortunately further inspiration descended on me during the singing of the Psalm, and I doubt if anyone knew of my predicament.

The new Vicar, John Duncan, was a 'leftie', and, since he had known of the Walls' difficulties and had made no move to help, I did not feel well disposed towards him. The following Sunday I arrived to take part in the clergy procession, and John met me and said he would rather I sat with the congregation. The tension between us blew up the following Remembrance Sunday. This coincided with the Russian invasion of Afghanistan. John defended this in his sermon. Were the Russians not justified in seeing themselves as encircled by the Americans? Was their action not simply defensive? I listened to these rhetorical questions murmuring to myself the answer, No. Nor was I alone in feeling the impropriety of the sermon to the occasion. One could repeatedly hear people walking out of the church and slamming the door as they went. Finally I got up and suggested that the sermon be finished in the church hall, where people could have a chance to respond. John concluded abruptly, but there was no discussion. I still feel very ill at ease at having interrupted a fellow preacher's sermon. John wrote saying that if we were to have any future relations I must write an apology in the parish paper, and I agreed to do this. But I still believe that if clergy feel called to comment on controversial political issues, they should allow opportunity for dissent.

Chapter 11

University of Birmingham

A university's primary task is to research and to teach its internal students; but many British universities have accepted the obligation to provide courses on the same level for such of the general public as wish to attend. The University of Birmingham had an Extramural Department (Latin *extra muros*, outside the walls), consisting of some thirty Staff Tutors in different subjects, whose task was to provide such courses across the West Midlands, which included Birmingham, Warwickshire, Worcestershire, Herefordshire, Shropshire, and south Staffordshire. I had now accepted to be the Staff Tutor in Theology over this area, and went to be instructed by Rundle Clark, the Deputy Director, as to how the job should be done. I emerged little wiser; I was to engage part-time tutors to teach theology courses in any towns or villages in which there was a demand; but it was by no means clear how I should set about this. He did vouchsafe three pieces of advice: one, always try to make a success of tonight's lecture; two, do not develop a specialism in a second subject; three, do not commit adultery with the wife of any of your colleagues. I followed the first, but did not keep the second of these, as I developed a strong interest in the Old Testament as well as the New. There was no great temptation over the third injunction.

Rundle, as he was known, was an amiably eccentric Egyptologist; he had a reputation as a lecturer, and I was advised to go and hear him, and see how the job was done. I did so, but was less impressed than I expected: some fifteen ladies of 50+ nodded through an account of Hatshepsut and other ancient Egyptian worthies; I was feeling that I could have been more interesting talking about St Paul. I could not, however, have competed with his final line: everyone sat up as he concluded with a reference to an erecto-phallic mummy.

I wanted to start the job by making a bit of a splash; and I thought of a format which might attract a public. I could pick a controversial subject and invite speakers of opposite opinions to speak for the two sides. My first choice was Papal Infallibility, and here I was fortunate in finding excellent speakers. Austin Farrer agreed generously to speak first, criticising the concept, and he was brilliant. He referred to two recent infallible papal decrees as 'a fact-factory going full blast'. Catholics expected Protestants to swallow the notion of infallibility, but this could only be done if the word was used, like our *Sovereign* Lady the Queen, or the German *Democratic* Republic—in other words, retaining the word, whilst emptying it of any meaning. The real value of infallibility was its edifying effect on Catholics; Austin compared it to King Ahab, who was struck by an arrow, and stayed up in his chariot till the going down of the sun, lest the children of Israel be scattered as sheep upon the mountainside. This was devastating, and no Catholic questioner disputed with Austin. I had the resource of the Oratory close by in Birmingham, and Father Dessain spoke for the Catholics, describing the milder position of Newman alongside the more aggressive one of Manning in the 1870s when the doctrine was promulgated. The lectures were well attended, and although they did not succeed in producing a crossing of swords as I had hoped, they set a precedent which I was able to continue successfully for more than a decade.

Austin also helped me with a second initiative, which was a two-day course for ministers and clergy, held in the Birmingham Diocesan Retreat House, Wadderton, near Blackwell. I had three speakers, Austin, the newly arrived philosopher of religion John Hick, and Bob Lambourne, a psychiatrist teaching Pastoral Studies in the Theology Department. About twenty people turned up, and both Austin and John were a great success. There were of course rooms for the lecturers to stay in the house, but to my surprise Austin insisted on driving back to Oxford each night, as his wife Kay was fragile, and made anxious by his absence. Bob was more of a worry; he sat through dinner next to me in ominous silence, and said at one point, 'It was a mistake for me to accept: I am not good at this kind of thing'. Nor was he: when I introduced him, the lecture lasted forty-five seconds. He did not like public speaking and had lost his nerve. I was grateful to the only Catholic priest who was attending, who immediately said, 'Thank you Doctor, that was most interesting', and posed a quite irrelevant question. This was just what the occasion required; the situation immediately changed from a lecture to a seminar, and seminar discussion was just what Bob was expert at leading. So we all went to bed happy.

Austin was most generous to me with his time when I came back from Hong Kong. I think he had some affection for me, though I was never in any sense a favourite pupil. But it is also true that he was feeling increasingly isolated. He had written a book of philosophy, *Finite and*

Infinite, which was regarded as brilliant but too difficult for most people to understand. He had also written two books which were well received on the Apocalypse, *A Rebirth of Images* (1949, his Bampton Lectures), and a commentary (1964). His books on Mark's Gospel, *A Study in St Mark* (1951), and *St Matthew and St Mark* (1954), and his article 'On Dispensing with Q', were regarded, however, in the profession as the work of a wayward genius. Austin disliked the tradition of young scholars researching for doctorates, and in consequence he had hardly any pupils to continue his work after him. One, Aileen Guilding, had written an interesting book about St John, and was Professor at Sheffield. But otherwise there was really only me, and he did his best to push me forward. There was a seminar at Oxford for New Testament scholars, and he asked them to invite me to contribute a paper. This was a major opportunity to show my ability, and I accepted with alacrity, although I was quite uncertain how I was to make use of it. At this point I had two pieces of luck: I noticed a book on the shelf which Clare had bought while reading for her English degree, Caroline Spurgeon's *Shakespeare's Imagery;* and I also lighted by accident on a book in the Extramural library, Feldman's *Parables and Similes of the Rabbis.* Both of these books were gifts from heaven. Professor Spurgeon drew a contrast between Shakespeare's use of images and that of his contemporaries, Marlowe, Bacon, Dekker and so on. Not only do these dramatists have their own preferred choice of images, as Marlowe is fond of celestial images, but also they treat them in personal ways, as when Shakespeare views a storm at sea as if from a cliff, while others imagine themselves on board the boat.

All this rang a bell in my mind: my work on the Lord's Prayer had suggested that both Matthew and Luke were prepared to put Jesus' supposed teaching in their own words. Now came the suggestion that they might have done the same thing with imagery, especially in the parables, which were Jesus' chief vehicle of teaching. It was well known that all the best parables come in Luke's Gospel, like the Good Samaritan and the Prodigal Son. The more I thought of it the more it seemed that each Synoptic Gospel had its own style of parable. Mark's parables were mostly agricultural: the Sower, the Seed Growing Secretly, and Mustard Seed. This was rather in line with Old Testament parables, which are said often to be about trees, 'from the cedar in Lebanon to the hyssop that grows out of the wall'. Matthew's parables are about people, mostly kings or wealthy merchants. Luke's parables, on the other hand, are about more down-to-earth characters: a prodigal son, an unjust steward, a widow, a beggar, a Samaritan. Feldman's book put an interesting gloss on this: he gave numerous examples of rabbinic parables, many of which compare God to a king or wealthy landowner. I therefore had a theme ready made for my Oxford seminar: the parables in the Gospels were not the parables of Jesus, as was assumed by almost everyone, including the authors of two of the best known books on the subject, C.H. Dodd in *The Parables of the Kingdom*, and J. Jeremias in *Parables of Jesus*: rather they were the creation of the evangelists, each of whom has produced instances in his own style. So I went well armed to Oxford, and as I hoped the paper was a great success. Even Professor Caird, who was not sympathetic to my ideas, commented appreciatively, 'Look at the observation': I had noticed a whole row of things which other scholars had missed, because they had assumed that the parables were Jesus' own handiwork, and had not thought of attributing them to secondary figures.

Chapter 12

THE SPEAKER'S LECTURERSHIP

The Oxford seminar was in many ways the turning point of my career. I sent the paper to Professor Sparks, and he agreed to publish it in the *JTS*. A few weeks later I had a letter from Austin: in the nineteenth century a group of Oxford scholars had published a volume for clergy, head teachers, etc, called *The Speaker's Commentary on Holy Scripture*; the book had sold well and made money, which was used to endow a Speaker's Lecturership in Biblical Studies, to be held by a distinguished visiting scholar, for three years, at six lectures a year. Austin was himself the Chairman of the Electors at the present time, and he suggested that I should apply for the post, carefully setting out my prospectus. He added, 'You will not get it, but it will give me a chance to praise your name in the seats of the mighty'. I decided to try my hand, but postponed sending in the application until I had written my prospectus. A fortnight later came a postcard, 'Do put in for the Speaker; the field of applicants is small'. As it happened things turned out to my advantage. There were two other applicants, George Caird, already a successful Oxford lecturer in NT, and James Barr, a distinguished Professor of Old Testament at Edinburgh. The first meeting of the Electors had to be cancelled as most of them were away on holiday; a second meeting was held some time later, and in the meantime my article had come out.

Opinion at the meeting swung back and forwards. To some Caird seemed the obvious candidate; he was an extremely popular lecturer at Oxford, who could fill the South School, some three hundred seats; a student told me, 'A Caird lecture is an experience'. Caird was not on the official lecturers' list, and was not paid for his lectures. Some of the Electors felt that giving him the Speaker's Lecturership would make up for this, while others felt that he already lectured too much. There may even have been some envy of his success among those who would be happy with an audience one-tenth of his size. The Professor of Hebrew, McHardie, proposed me. Before the meeting Austin had sent round a postcard: no doubt the Electors were familiar with the writings of Barr and Caird, but I was less known, and they might like to consult my recent article in the *JTS*. Two of the Electors were visitors from Cambridge, who were content to see the Oxford Electors argue it out, so long as they could see fair play. Hedley Sparks, the remaining Elector, would have preferred Barr, and argued the case against me. My thesis was too far-reaching, and he doubted if I was sufficiently familiar with the Rabbis to defend it. Austin said that if my thesis was true it was important, and deserved a hearing; in his own words, 'I had to do some hard swearing about your competence in Hebrew'. Sparks' hesitation was fully justified; I had at the time enrolled in a Hebrew class, and had read the Hebrew Bible as far as the thirty-fifth chapter of Genesis. Austin wrote to me afterwards, 'I held him to it', and in the end he accepted that I should have it. Austin wrote to congratulate me, concluding, 'In this matter the greater part of the credit should be ascribed to the Divine Providence: first, for putting me in the Chair; second, for sending most of the Electors on holiday; third, for bringing your article out in the nick of time; and fourth, for moving the unpredictable heart of the Professor of Hebrew'. All was still not quite plain sailing; the letter offering me the post was misdirected to the Theology Department. Three weeks later a further letter was sent enquiring whether I wanted the post; and this time I did receive the letter.

Austin advised me not to fix the dates of my lectures with the Registry; he would arrange with the dons' seminar to make my lectures the subject of their meetings. He would take the chair, and if there were any unfair questions, he would rule them out of order. It was later agreed that my lectures should be held in my old college, Trinity, and that the first one should be on the 21st January 1969. I had just received a further letter from him, and was reading it, when Clare came in with a copy of the Times in her hand. It announced that Austin had died of a heart attack, and even included a full-scale obituary; the date was 30th December, 1968, and he was just sixty-four. I could hardly believe it; the letter from him in my hand, written just two days before, seemed to contradict the evidence in the paper. My sense of loss was doubly acute: first, that of Austin himself, so long admired as a person; and then, the loss of the support and guidance he would have given me in the taxing months ahead. I felt naked indeed. Yet on reflection I might have been warned. Austin was a selfless man: he was fond of Kay his wife, but she suffered from severe depression, and he had had to give her a lot of support. At the same time he was a devoted Warden of Keble College. Building work had been needed on the top of the College tower, and Austin had climbed a sixty-foot ladder to inspect the work. When the College library was being moved, Austin went up and down staircases carrying armfuls of books. It was no wonder that his heart was under strain.

So I went to deliver my first Speaker on 21st January, without the protection of Austin's chairmanship and the support of his subsequent comments. The meetings were held in the Danson Room, a comfortable modern lecture room in Trinity. The first meeting was attended by about sixty people, including most of the New Testament dons; the reception was friendly, aided perhaps by sympathy at the evident misfortune of my having so suddenly been deprived of my mentor. There were some telling questions from the learned, which I did my best to answer. Caird was there, and remarked loudly (and inaccurately), 'But first he will have to disprove Q'. Henry Chadwick asked a courteous but menacing question, which I answered rather inadequately. I had arranged to speak principally about St Matthew, and to cover the Gospel in eight lectures a year. The attendance sagged, both in numbers and in quality, but the overall result was sufficiently successful for my tenure to be extended by two years, so that I could also cover St Luke's Gospel.

The first few lectures covered material I had already well in hand. An extended version of my parables argument was a considerable success; and I was able to develop Caroline Spurgeon's images theme to cover a wider area of Jesus' teaching in Matthew. For instance, the Gospels contain a number of double animal images: 'Be ye wise as serpents and harmless as doves'; 'You strain out a gnat but swallow a camel'; 'Give not that which is holy to the dogs and cast not your pearls before swine'. There are ten of these double animal images in the Gospels, and all of them are in Matthew; this seems cogent evidence that they were created, not by Jesus, but by Matthew himself. I drew a second, similar argument from the striking rhythms which again recur in Matthew's Gospel only. The sentence quoted above about serpents and doves has the same rhythm as the OT, 'Can the Ethiopian change his skin, or the leopard its spots?' Such sentences have two parts, but the same verb is used without repetition in the second as in the first (here 'change'). I needed a name for such rhythms, and invented the name 'pardics' for this, after the Greek word *pardos*, a leopard.

My problem came with the general structure of Matthew's Gospel. It is widely accepted that the Gospel consists of a series of incidents, mostly healings, broken by five Discourses: the Sermon on the Mount (chs. 5–7), the Mission Discourse (ch. 10), the Harvest Parables (ch. 13), a Church Law Discourse (chs. 18–19), and the Discourse on the End (chs. 24–25). Some scholars have suggested that Matthew had in mind a parallel to the five books of the Law; but the fit is not good, and I found the idea unconvincing. A solution came to me, as to Archimedes, in my bath; in the form of another question, What did Matthew have in mind as the purpose of his book? It can hardly have been to sell it in a bookshop, and the general tone of the Gospel suggests that it was written to be read aloud in church. But he couldn't have meant all twenty-eight chapters to be read aloud at one sitting, and an alternative occurred to me as much more likely. The book could be divided into so many units, to be read serially, one each Sunday. Chapter 28, Matthew's last chapter, the Resurrection story, could suitably be read on Easter Day. If the book were written to be read as a cycle, his first chapters would then follow. These consist of a series of stories, most of which he signs off with a formula, such as, 'All this came to pass that it might be fulfilled which was spoken by the prophet...': Jesus' Birth, the Wise Men, the Flight into Egypt, the Baptism, the Temptations, the First Disciples. After these comes Matthew's first Discourse, the Sermon on the Mount. Now the coincidence here seemed very striking. Jesus was killed at Passover time; seven weeks after Passover came the Jewish Feast of Pentecost. This was celebrated as the occasion that Moses received the Law on Mount Sinai; and here, seven sections after Easter, we have Jesus giving a new version of the Law on the mountain. He says, 'Think not that I came to destroy the Law and Prophets; I came not to destroy but to fulfil', and he goes on to contrast the old Ten Commandments with '...but I say unto you'. In other words Matthew appears to be providing a story to be read out in church each Sunday, and for the Jewish festivals, there were especially suitable discourses of Jesus. The Gospel was designed to provide readings for the whole year.

The further Discourses were also appropriate: to Jews, New Year was a feast celebrating the Kingdom of God, and in ch. 10 there follows Matthew's second Discourse, the sending of the Apostles to proclaim the coming of the Kingdom. Tabernacles was a feast celebrating the harvest, and in ch. 13 comes the third Discourse, the Parables of the Harvest. Between these two passages comes Jesus' reproach of the cities where he had preached for their failure to repent, in contrast to the men of Nineveh who did repent at the preaching of Jonah. This would fall ideally for Yom Kippur, the annual Fast, when Israel was to repent of its sins, the 10th of Tishri, between New Year on the 1st and Tabernacles from the 15th to the 22nd; the Book of Jonah is the traditional prophetic reading for the Fast. Matthew 17 presents Jesus transfigured in light, a suitable theme for Hanukkah, the Feast of Lights, and this then leads on to the Fourth Discourse, chs. 18–19. Matthew 22 brings us to the Royal Wedding Feast; one guest attends without a wedding garment, and is cast out into outer darkness. The parable would serve well for a Christian celebration of Purim, when King Ahasuerus gave a dinner for his new wife Esther, and the unworthy guest Haman, who has been plotting the liquidation of the Jewish people, is cast out and hanged on his own gibbet. Matthew 24–25, the last Discourse, warns the Church of the coming of its Lord at Passover. Mark gives substantially the same discourse in ch. 13, and concludes, 'What I say to you, I say to all, Watch: for you know not when your Lord cometh, late or at midnight, or cockcrow, or early' (i.e. dawn). This follows the progress of the Passion narrative: Jesus comes at evening for the Passover meal; after this he takes the disciples to Gethsemane, where three times he says, 'Could you not watch with me one hour?' Jesus is then arrested: Peter denies him at cockcrow, and he is tried by Pilate at dawn. The fourth century pilgrim, Egeria, describes the Vigil kept by the Jerusalem church on Passover night with Gospel readings at the different locations mentioned in the story; the church then kept Passover with an adoration of the Cross. The Gospel divides the day into a series of watches, the trial at dawn, the crucifixion at the third hour, darkness from the sixth hour, Jesus' death at the ninth hour, his burial before sundown. So much detail would be well explained if the church was already keeping vigil through the full day of expectation of Jesus' coming.

This seemed to give a convincing account of the structure of the Gospel; but I needed evidence that at some point it was actually used like this. Egeria visited Jerusalem in 381 CE, but this is three centuries after Matthew, and I could do with much earlier evidence. I thought I had found this in an early manuscript, Alexandrinus, which divides Matthew's text into sections which roughly corresponded to my divisions—including a single section for the whole Sermon on the Mount. I was very pleased with my solution to the structure of the Gospel, and was much disappointed to have it punctured in the question time after my lecture. Hedley Sparks had examined carefully the Table of sections in Alexandrinus which I had prepared, and he commented, 'Your reading of the Sermon on the Mount covers 107 verses of the Gospel, whereas other readings, like the Woman with the Issue of Blood, consist of only two verses. Is not this very implausible?' He was right: it was very implausible, and I ought to have noticed it. I would have liked to answer, 'The Woman with the Issue of Blood is described as part of the Raising of Jairus' Daughter, and taken together they comprize four verses'. But even this would have left a big disparity with the Sermon, and it would mean abandoning my claim that the Alexandrinus sections were intended to mark readings. I had wanted them as early evidence of my reading pattern, and my overall picture would have seemed much weaker if I had to divide Matthew up myself to fit my theory.

It was a big disappointment that so original and comprehensive an explanation should fail to gain scholarly approval; and I still think that it provides the most satisfying answer to the problem. It is widely agreed now that a Gospel was intended for public reading in church. Dennis Nineham thought that a Gospel was a collection of anecdotes about Jesus, from which the preacher was at liberty to select to fit his sermon. Morna Hooker thought that the whole of Mark might be read at a single sitting, to create a major impact. But Jews did not treat their Scriptures like this: they read the Law serially; if the reading finished at Gen. 17 one Sabbath, it would start at Gen. 18 the next. So it would be much more likely that a Jewish Christian like Matthew would expect his Gospel to be read serially. Also his book fits the pattern of worship at the Festivals round the year, with a discourse for each feast on the appropriate subject. This fitted too neatly to be accidental, and the Jewish Festal cycle had been established for centuries.

I often had occasion to expound my theory to later audiences, and I omitted the Alexandrinus hypothesis when I did so, as it did not provide the support which I needed. The last occasion was at the Symposium on my work held in Johns Hopkins University, Baltimore, many years later, in February 2000. Questions were then asked by two heavyweight scholars. John Kloppenborg, a Canadian, commented, 'The argument depends on the Jewish Festivals being in use in Matthew's time: but your appeal to the Fast of 9th Ab is inapplicable, since the rabbis do not mention the Fast till a hundred years later'. This was a much easier question than Sparky's years before, because although the rabbis do not refer to the Fast, it is mentioned by the prophet Zechariah about 500 BCE. The other questioner was Krister Stendhal, a Swedish American Bishop, who was a doyen of American NT scholarship. He commented, 'Scholars are generally agreed that Matthew was dependent on Mark's Gospel. Is it not extraordinary that Matthew should have written his Gospel in the way you have described if Mark had no basis of this kind?' This was a problem I had thought of for myself, and was ready with my answer: 'In my view Mark was written exactly as Matthew was, to be read section by section round the year. The only difference is that whereas Matthew began his account with the Sunday after Easter, Mark began his from the Jewish New Year, the natural beginning to an annual cycle for a community with Jewish roots. Jews celebrated New Year as an occasion for rejoicing at the coming of the Kingdom of God, in the spirit of humble repentance. Hence the suitability of Mark's opening paragraph, in which

John the Baptist proclaims, 'Repent; for the Kingdom of God is at hand".
So in my view both Gospels were written to be read round the Church's
year, but beginning at different points.

When my years of Speaker's Lectures were complete, I sent the
manuscript of the Matthew section to the SPCK in hope of publication.
The editor was willing in principle, but required a two-hundred pound
subsidy, and would give me no royalty on the first edition. I was able to
secure a grant for the £200 from the Hort Fund; and stipulated that if I
received no royalty on the first edition I should have fifteen percent on
subsequent editions. The question then arose of a title for the book, and
I adopted the not very beautiful, but accurate, *Midrash and Lection in
Matthew*. I was arguing two theses. One of these was, as I have explained,
that the Gospel was written as a series of lections, to be read out in
church. The other was that Matthew was a creative author, elaborating
the tradition which he had received from Mark. Similar elaboration was
the technique used by the Chronicler in elaborating the narrative of
Samuel-Kings. He twice uses the Hebrew word *midrash* to signify this.
The root meaning of the word is an enquiry, but in time it was taken
up by Jewish authors to signify a commentary on Scripture, citing the
opinions of earlier rabbis. Some purist critics objected to my choice of
this word which had come to have an established meaning so different
from how I was using it myself; but I felt that if the Chronicler so used
it, it was open to me to do likewise, meaning by it an elaboration or
embroidery, rather than a commentary. Furthermore, in the 1960s and
1970s scholars used the term in my sense quite widely. The book was
published in 1974, and it received some friendly reviews. I extended the
lectionary side of the argument to Mark and Luke in a further volume,
The Evangelists' Calendar, which was published in 1978.

My case against Q was incomplete without an exposition of Luke's
handling of Matthew; and in the two-year extension to my Speaker's
Lectures I turned to expound the Gospel of Luke. I revised this at leisure
in the 1980s, and it was published in 1989 under the title *Luke: A New
Paradigm*. Paradigm is a term that had been introduced by a philosopher
Thomas Kuhn in 1962, (expanded version 1970), in a discussion of the
process by which scientific knowledge is advanced. It was unlikely that
an innovative theorist would reach the full truth in one bound, but it was
normal for an outline, or paradigm, to be proposed, which would itself
contain a number of subsidiary hypotheses. If the paradigm became
generally accepted, it tended to be used uncritically, and anomalies
would be easily overlooked. A change of perspective would arise only
when it was realized that the accepted position was defective, and a shift

of paradigm would result. This seemed to me to have been the case with the Synoptic Problem. The standard solution had simply been the picture accepted by the learned for more than a hundred years, and anomalies which should have raised doubts about it had been broadly neglected. Whereas the standard paradigm for Luke's Gospel supposes that Luke drew not only on Mark but also on two sources now lost to us—Q, which was also known to Matthew, and L, which was Luke's private source—I was supposing that Luke knew Matthew's Gospel as well as Mark's, and that the Q and L material was nothing else but Luke's elaboration of what he found in Matthew.

My exposition of Luke began with a renewed onslaught on Q. I opened the book with a revised version of my Edinburgh paper of a decade before, 'The House Built on Sand'; and added further arguments on the contradictions involved in the Q concept. But a further important topic was the recurrent features to be found in Luke's story-telling. Luke has a considerable cluster of characteristic traits which are to be found not only in his parables but also in the narratives of the Infancy and Resurrection of Jesus, and on into the Acts. I have already commented that the heroes of Luke's parables are, unlike those of Matthew, low-cast people: dishonest judges and stewards, women, widows, a beggar, a Samaritan, a sinner. But these people also behave in Lucan ways. They act with promptitude and alacrity: they get up and go, they run, they proceed with haste, they sit down quickly. Also we see into their hearts. They soliloquize: 'I cannot dig, to beg I am ashamed', 'I will go to my father and will say to him...'. They ruminate: 'Did not our hearts burn within us?' They open their souls to us, in prayer: 'O God, I thank thee that I am not as other men are...'. Then there are the doubled vocatives: when Jesus addresses his followers in tones of mild remonstrance, he names them twice: 'Simon, Simon...', 'Martha, Martha...', 'Saul, Saul...'. After such an opening Jesus is liable to ask a question to which the disciple can only give one answer, and that an embarrassed one. One Pharisee is told the parable of the two debtors, and another that of the Good Samaritan: and to each such a question is asked. The former of these parables is Lucan in another way. One debtor owes five hundred dinars, and the other fifty, a proportion of ten to one; whereas Matthew has a master entrusting his money to three of his servants, Luke's master has ten servants, and the most successful of these is rewarded with authority over ten cities. Similarly, the divine initiative often involves two earthly recipients, and Luke takes pains to see they are both properly warned in advance. Gabriel tells Zechariah that his wife is to bear a child, John the Baptist; and the Archangel goes on to tell Mary that she is to be the mother of Christ. She is to go and visit her aged relative, and the Visitation of Elizabeth then follows. In the same way Cornelius is told to go and see Peter in Acts ch. 10, and at the same time Peter is warned in a vision that Cornelius is coming.

The second half of my work on Luke was devoted to a detailed commentary. Up till then it had always been objected to Farrer's theory that Luke could not plausibly have produced his Gospel simply by reworking Matthew (and Mark). For example, Matthew ch.1 describes the Annunciation of the birth of Jesus to Joseph; what can Luke be supposed to have done with this, since his first chapter describes the Annunciation not to Joseph but to Mary? I do not think this question is unanswerable. If Luke thought that God was courteous enough to tell Joseph what was happening to Mary, he might well think it would be even more courteous to let Mary herself into the secret. Furthermore, Matthew begins his Gospel with two lists of Joseph's ancestors, one going as far as David, the other back to Abraham. It might well seem believable then that Luke has felt that he could build his own account of the Annunciations out of the biblical promises to David in Isaiah and those to Abraham in Genesis. Luke follows Mark in portraying John the Baptist as the forerunner of Jesus, and his portrait of John's conception is built squarely on the Abraham tradition. The wonderful conception of John is then transcended by the miraculous conception of Jesus from a virgin as Isaiah prophesied. Thus the whole Lucan story can suitably be derived from a Lucan reading of Mark and Matthew; and I drew similar conclusions for the whole Lucan Gospel, showing that we can dispense with both Q and L in our reading of Luke.

The commentary was a *tour de force*. I had to take on all the standard defenders of the Two-Source Theory—Schürmann, Schmidt, Jeremias, and others—and I felt that I had made my case. The book was well reviewed in the major journals, especially by John Muddiman, and was later reissued in paperback, a rare accolade from JSOT Press, especially for such a long and technical study. It remains my best piece of work, and a challenge to which traditionalists have yet to respond.

Chapter 13

The Synoptic Problem

Soon after my return from Hong Kong in 1966, my friend John Sweet invited me to Cambridge to a meeting of the Society of New Testament Studies, a society to which I was elected a member in the following year, and in which much of my activities were to be concentrated. The Society was an international body, its proper name, *Studiorum Novi Testamenti Societas*, being in Latin to emphasize the fact; it consisted of about 700 scholars from all over the world, and held its meetings annually, each year by invitation to a university in a different country. With so many learned men and women at each meeting it was perilous to raise one's voice at the plenary sessions, and I wisely kept quiet for quite a few years; but in the mornings the Society divided into seminars of twenty to thirty members apiece to consider special areas, and I opted to join such a seminar on the Synoptic Problem.

The Problem concerns the origin and relationship of the Gospels of Matthew, Mark and Luke, which take the same view (Greek syn-optic, viewed together), of the story of Jesus. Mark tells this story in 660 verses, mostly of narrative, from the preaching of John the Baptist to Jesus' Passion and Resurrection. Matthew and Luke have this same narrative, in the same order, and nearly in the same words; but they also contain a good amount of Jesus' teaching. About 200 verses of this teaching are common to Matthew and Luke, often in identical wording; but both have a certain amount of additional material peculiar to themselves.

There have been three main groups of theories to explain this situation. In the late 1700s a German scholar called Griesbach suggested that Matthew wrote first and Mark last, an abbreviation of the other two Gospels. This theory, which does not really explain why Mark should behave in this way, was virtually given up in the 1830s. I was most surprised to find therefore that there was a strong following for it in the Seminar. The leading figure among these, mostly American, scholars was a friendly man called Bill Farmer. He was an obsessive: he was totally convinced that Griesbach was correct, and I never knew him say a sentence about any other subject. He believed in a conspiracy theory: other scholars were determined to suppress Griesbach by fair means or foul; and when I was Chairman of the Seminar he accused me of refusing fair treatment because I ruled that I could not give the whole programme of the Seminar to considering a recent book supporting him. There was one Englishman among this group, an elderly Benedictine monk called Bernard Orchard; he was a significant figure because he had access to considerable private funding from a Catholic family connected with C. and A. Modes, and he used this money to pay for a number of conferences on the Problem, some of which I attended.

Farmer's pertinacity and Orchard's funding achieved more than their theory deserved. Farmer gathered a considerable group of scholars to support him, and they succeeded in giving the impression that if one did not accept the Standard Solution the only viable alternative was Griesbach. Thus for a period of years the Farrer theory was sidelined, and as I thought that Griesbach was so obviously wrong I underestimated the amount of harm which the Griesbachians were doing me. Farmer himself regularly assumed that because I did not follow the Standard Solution I must therefore agree with him, and inevitably this resulted in my being tarred with his brush. It is only in quite recent times that the Griesbachian movement has virtually collapsed, and my theory is now regarded as the major alternative, even in the USA.

From the 1830s there came to be a second, and much more widely accepted, hypothesis: Mark was the first Gospel to be written, and Matthew and Luke had both known it and produced expanded versions of it. The 200 verses of teaching which they shared were supposed to come from a common lost source, which in time came to be called Q, from *Quelle*, the German for a source: just as they both had access to Mark, so they both had access to this now lost document. In addition, Matthew had access to a private source, known as M, and Luke to a private source known as L. This theory became so widely accepted that it is known as the Standard Theory, though often called by the muddling name the Two-Source Theory. The Standard Theory was developed by many scholars in the nineteenth century, and was further expounded by British scholars mostly at Oxford in the twentieth. Chief among these was B.H.Streeter, whose book, *The Four Gospels*, was published in 1924. The Theory went virtually unchallenged until 1957, when Austin Farrer wrote an article, 'On Dispensing with Q'. Farrer's central argument was an appeal to the principle set out in the Middle Ages by William of Occam, 'Entities should not be multiplied beyond what is necessary': this principle, which is accepted as a rule of thumb in almost all research work, would rule out the Q hypothesis. Since Luke wrote later than Matthew, the 200 common verses could be explained as taken over by Luke direct from Matthew.

I was the only member of the Seminar to defend a third theory, which had been proposed by Austin Farrer: Mark wrote first, and Matthew and Luke both produced second editions of Mark; but Luke read Matthew as well as Mark, and either transcribed or adapted those passages of Matthew which other scholars ascribe to Q. The main defender of the Standard Theory was a stocky Belgian, Frans Neirynck, the Professor of Leuven. Neirynck was a formidable and ambitious man. He meant to make Leuven the European centre for the study of the Gospels, but there were difficulties in his way. Belgium is divided into French and Flemish speakers, and only a few years before, this division had split the University, the Flemish speakers retaining the site of the mediaeval university, while the French speakers decamped to Louvain-la-Neuve. But Flemish is not an international language, and if Leuven was to attract able students from other countries the teaching would have to be in English, as a *lingua franca*. Neirynck prevailed on the University authorities to have all courses in Theology taught in English, and he succeeded in attracting good students from both Britain and America. He established a journal in New Testament study for his university, the *Ephemerides theologicae lovanienses*, many of the articles in which he wrote himself; there were also a series of monographs under the initials *B.E.T.L.(Bibliotheca...)*. Neirynck's Tuesday seminars were ruled with an iron discipline. He would collect every book and article on a New Testament topic published the previous week, and allot them to the different members of the seminar, and the following Tuesday each one was required to contribute an outline and a critique of the relevant work. But Neirynck had also read all this material himself, and anyone whose digest and critique were inadequate was exposed to ruthless humiliation. This wide reading coupled with his keen powers of exegesis and a sharp forensic skill made him a formidable adversary; but I was soon able to contest points with him, and I found him fair-minded and kindly. In fact most of the significant interchanges in the Seminar were between him and me, for he respected me as holding a consistent and defensible position, although naturally he thought it wrong. I was also surprised to discover that although he seemed at first to lack a sense of humour he was quite happy for me to make gentle fun of him. He published a collection of his articles in a volume of *B.E.T.L.* which I was sent for review. It included one essay in which he exposed a little-known scholar for plagiarism; and I commented, 'Those who had come to think that their sins would never be proclaimed by the Archangel from the housetops may be surprised to find his surrogate in the Poirot-esque figure of the Professor of Leuven'. A second volume, edited by his junior colleague van Segbroeck, was published with a green jacket wrapper adorned with a mediaeval drawing of St John dictating to the Beloved Disciple. I wrote, 'The matter is well symbolized by the handsome green cover now added to the normally austere *B.E.T.L.* format: a bearded Neirynck receives the word of truth from the right hand of the Almighty (top right), while an alarmed Van Segbroeck sits (bottom left), prepared to inscribe it. Both scholars are beatified with Q-shaped haloes'. I was pleased that Neirynck appreciated the joke.

The atmosphere in the Seminar was friendly. At one session Joe Tyson, a large man, presented a paper in support of Griesbach arguing for the significance of a certain word being used four times in one block of text and ninety-one times in another. I responded that there were reasons for this, and suggested a parallel; if a man were found to have kissed two women, one four times and one ninety-one times, it might be that one was his daughter and the other his wife, and we should not think him a sex maniac. It was understood in the Society that members could speak English, French, and German, but in our group there was a quiet French-speaking Belgian, Père Denis, who was left quite at sea by Tyson's Texan English. So I provided an impromptu French translation of my analogy: 'On vous dit une petite histoire au sujet d'un tel homme qui a embracé deux femmes, l'une quatre fois, l'autre quatre-vingt-et-onze fois...' This was greeted with cheers and ironic demands that I provide a further translation into German.

During 1975 I became increasingly frustrated by the lack of progress. Scholars were content to assume the truth of the Standard Theory, and to ignore Austin's appeal to Occam's principle; what was necessary was a cogent argument that Luke was using a copy of Matthew's Gospel. I had one lead for this purpose: as Matthew and Luke were both re-writing the narrative sections of Mark, naturally any changes they made to Mark's text were sometimes identical. These changes varied very much in length. Sometimes they might extend to five or six verses, as when both later evangelists add John Baptist's Sermon to Mark's account of his preaching (six verses). Often it is only a few words which are added, and when this is the case they are referred to as Minor Agreements (MA), a term coined in 1909 by an Oxford scholar, Sir John Hawkins, who had made a list of the more striking of them, as representing embarrassments to the Standard Theory. It was easy to explain the major agreements: Matthew and Luke might both be drawing on a passage from Q. But the Minor Agreements would cause more difficulty. An example would be the Sadducees' Question in Mark 12. Here Mark writes, 'Last (*eschaton*) of all the woman died'. Matthew and Luke both change his *eschaton* to *husteron* ('later'). This is interesting: Matthew likes the word *husteron*, which he uses six times elsewhere in the Gospel, whereas Luke never uses the word elsewhere, either in his Gospel or in the Acts. An obvious explanation for this could be that he had read the word in Matthew's Gospel and just copied it down. It occurred to me during the Seminar discussions that a number of these MAs were significant in this way: they were characteristic of Matthew's way of writing, but uncharacteristic of Luke's; and this suggested that Luke had not made these changes independently, but had taken them from Matthew. Even a single instance of non-Lucan style in an MA would, if sufficiently striking, seem to show that Luke knew Matthew; but as I went carefully through the texts I found no fewer than twelve such passages which seemed to me to be instances of this point.

During the winter I had a phone call from Robin Barbour, the Secretary of the SNTS, saying that the Committee had decided to devote one session of the 1976 Meeting to a discussion of the Synoptic Problem. Accordingly he had written to Neirynck, who was now Chairman of the Seminar, asking him to choose a passage of Mark's Gospel and to propose three members of the Seminar to represent three different synoptic theories. Neirynck had been ill ('poor chap'), so Robin's request had not been quickly answered; he had now, however, suggested that he himself would defend the Standard Theory, that Bill Farmer should speak for the Griesbach hypothesis, and that I should defend the Farrer Theory. Was I willing to do this? I was indeed, since I wanted nothing more than to expound Austin's view to the whole Society. Everything, however, would depend upon which passage Neirynck had proposed; my heart was in my mouth, hoping that he might have selected one of my twelve sections. I ought to have been consulted about the selection, but the truth was that Neirynck had had a cold ('poor chap'), and found it convenient to postpone answering letters. But fortunately for me he had chosen the first verses of Mark ch.16, and these were the last of my chosen passages. So I might hope to make my case effectively.

Mark ch.16 tells the story of the women's visit to Jesus' tomb on Easter morning. He begins, 'Extremely early'. Matthew makes this more specific, 'After Sabbath as it was dawning into the first day of the week'; he uses the Greek *epiphoskein*, derived from the noun *phos*, light, from which we get our 'photography'. Luke prefaces this with the story of Jesus' burial by Joseph of Arimathea; he concludes this, 'It was the Day of Preparation and Sabbath was dawning'. The surprising thing here is that Luke uses the same verb *epiphoskein* as Matthew does in the story following. The Jewish Sabbath begins at sundown, a fact which Luke knows perfectly well, and is implied by his 'Day of Preparation'—i.e. Jesus had been crucified on the Friday and was being buried before Sabbath began. So Sabbath does not 'dawn', rather it begins by the day darkening as evening draws on. Luke has slipped into using a word with light in its root, and the only likely explanation for this is that he was influenced by Matthew's use of the same verb for the real dawn of Easter Day.

The debate was held at the SNTS Meeting in Duke University, North Carolina, in August 1976. I was disappointed to find that it was scheduled for 2.30 in the afternoon; mornings are hard work at the SNTS, and many members put their feet up after lunch. But in fact I need not have worried; the tiered hall was full to the doors. Neirynck spoke first. He had chosen the passage because some verses of it were discussed in a recent article, which I had not read. He had not noticed the cardinal point to which I was going to refer. Bill Farmer spoke second; he produced the standard Griesbach explanation that Mark abbreviated the other two Gospels when they agreed. This explained nothing, and his paper had little impact. So the way was open for me; I explained the striking coincidence of the use of *epiphoskein*, and sketched the rather lame explanations offered by other scholars. One of these was the respected Scottish Professor Matthew Black, who was sitting in the front row. When the question session began, I had an easy time. Neither Neirynck nor Farmer could puncture my argument, and there were no searching questions from the floor. The only person who did speak was Matthew Black, who unwisely attempted to defend the explanation he had offered in print; this brought down on his head a flood of contradiction in three languages, and I was left feeling triumphant. Robin Wilson, my old opponent at the Oxford Conference, was now Editor of *New Testament Studies*, the Society's journal, and he offered to publish all three of our papers. But in the event the other two withdrew and I alone had my piece in print, alongside the article in which I expounded my other eleven crucial instances; I called this paper 'On Putting Q to the Test'.

Soon after this a group of British scholars decided to float the idea of an annual conference of British NT specialists. This was planned at a meeting in London, to which I was invited, and I offered to give a paper. This was received in an atmosphere far different from that which I had enjoyed at Duke. This was largely my own fault: hitherto I had concentrated my studies on the Gospels, especially Matthew and Luke, but I wanted to be a scholar of the New Testament rather than just of the Gospels, so I wrote my paper about St Paul. This was rash, for I did not know the Pauline texts as I did the Gospels, nor had I read much of the enormous literature on the Apostle. And those present included Jimmy Dunn, Paddy Best, Morna Hooker, David Catchpole, Colin Hickling, and Margaret Thrall. These were almost all Pauline specialists, and they made hay of my amateur offering. They did not wish to be unkind, but I had volunteered the paper, and it would be helpful neither to me nor to the subject to pretend that my argument was convincing. As questions and hostile comments rained down, I began to experience a splitting headache, and after a while was reduced to saying that I could not carry on. I was encouraged by the kindness of David and Colin, who came to my aid with tea and unspoken sympathy; but I felt completely demoralized and defeated. I came to regard this unhappy incident as my 'Ulua'. [In the sixteenth century the Spaniards had the monopoly of the profitable trade between Europe and South America. In 1569 two small English vessels, commanded by Hawkins and Drake, sailed to the West Indies hoping for a share of the trade. They anchored in a West Indian island called San Juan de Ulua, where they were ambushed by much larger Spanish ships. The two English vessels limped home with decimated crews. But the lesson was learned: ten years later Drake sailed up the west coast of Peru, taking and destroying every Spanish vessel he met. Hawkins persuaded the Queen to build larger ships for the Royal Navy, with better guns; and it was these which pursued the Armada down the Channel and drove them to the North Atlantic and their destruction. I also learned something from the occasion and was later able to recover my reputation.]

The annual British NT Conference was duly established, and in 1978 I offered to host the meeting in Birmingham, and the conference was a success, both in itself and for me personally. Jimmy Dunn had been elected President, but he was unable to attend. This was a pity, because the opening paper was a critique of one of his ideas. The speaker, Prof. Anthony Hanson of Nottingham, was an unpretentious man who thought that NT scholars took themselves too seriously. His antidote was to compose appalling limericks on the spur of the moment, and he opened his talk with one such on a young fellow called Goulder. Most scholars believe that Paul thought that Jesus had existed in heaven before he became a man on earth, but Dunn had disputed this; Hanson's paper took his arguments to pieces effectively, and we missed our President's reply.

The second evening the paper was on a subject much closer to my own interests: it was on 'Streeter's handling of the Minor Agreements'. I have noted above that when Matthew and Luke agree in their changes to Mark it often looks as if Luke knew Matthew's Gospel, and this is inconvenient for the Standard Theory. Streeter's *The Four Gospels* is a defence of a version of the Standard Theory, and he had felt it necessary to counter these embarrassing Agreements; so he had devoted a whole chapter to explaining away twenty of them, beginning from some of the more easy ones and ending with the most difficult. Our speaker, who was my old sparring partner from the Oxford Conference, Robin Wilson, had not planned the timing of his paper well, and starting from Streeter's first example, was able to get only to the seventeenth. I was delighted by the paper, which exposed much of Streeter's special pleading; but I had read the chapter carefully and I knew that the paper had not reached the last, and most obviously feeble, argument. During the question time there was silence: most of the audience were subscribers to the Standard Theory, and were not pleased to have it shot to pieces by Wilson in this way. But I was not prepared to leave matters there. I said I was surprised that the speaker had not discussed Streeter's twentieth instance, which was the most scandalous of all. After Jesus' Trial, he is blindfolded, and in Mark mockers say to him, 'Prophesy!' Matthew and Luke alike add the following five (Greek) words, 'Who is it that smote you?' The Greek for 'smote' is *paiein*, a word which neither of them uses elsewhere. The Standard Hypothesis expressly excludes any version of the Passion narrative having been in Q. It therefore seems likely that Luke copied the words in from Matthew. To avoid this conclusion, Streeter suggests that the words were not originally in Matthew's Gospel, but that a later scribe copied them into Matthew from Luke. I was able to show that this was a piece of jiggery-pokery, and to be based on sheer speculation: the words were missing from Matthew in no Greek manuscript, nor in any of the versions, Latin, Syriac, Coptic, or other, nor in any citation from the Fathers. I was particularly pleased to be able to make this point, as among those attending was Neville Birdsall, my colleague in the Theology Department at Birmingham, himself a manuscript expert. He had often been rather offhand with me, and it was a pleasure to see him stand up and say that to his surprise he had to endorse my claim. The conference ended with a Business Meeting, at which I was asked to send a friendly message to our missing President. Encouraged by Hanson's example, I produced this limerick:

> We salute our friend James from a distance;
> But Anthony Hanson's insistence
>   Convinced everyone
>   That we haven't quite Dunn
> With the doctrine of Christ's pre-existence.

Chapter 14

The Myth of God Incarnate

Soon after I came to Birmingham, in 1967, John Hick joined the Theology
Department as H.G. Wood Professor; he was a philosopher of religion,
with a special interest in non-Christian religions. John was a clear-headed
man with advanced liberal opinions, which made him an attractive
teacher and speaker. He had previously taught at Princeton in America
and had been in trouble with his Presbyterian colleagues, some of whom
banded together to try to prevent him preaching in their churches. John
survived these attacks, and brought to Birmingham a reputation for bold
unorthodoxy. He immediately made a difference to the Department by
sponsoring a weekly seminar at which attendance and the offering of
papers was open to all. I used to attend, and quite soon was accepted to
give two papers; one of these, suggesting natural explanations for the
traditions of Jesus' resurrection, struck John as interesting and perhaps
significant. He asked me to lunch with him, and we became friends. John
was a pacifist, who had served in the War with the Friends' Ambulance
Unit, and he was an enthusiastic member of the Labour Party; I shared
neither of these convictions, but I admired his open-minded critique
of traditional Christian orthodoxy, and we became easy allies. After a
couple of years I became interested in the problem of how Jesus came to
be thought of as divine, and I read a paper to John's seminar suggesting
the novel hypothesis that the idea came from Christians in Samaria. Acts
recorded that a Samaritan called Simon believed himself to be the Power
of God, and John's Gospel reports the Jews as accusing Jesus of being a
Samaritan. This Simon became a figure of scandal in the second century.
He settled in Rome, and proclaimed himself to be God's Favoured One.
The Latin for this is Faustus, and he becomes demonized in subsequent
Christian tradition. John was impressed with my paper, and asked what
I would do with it; I replied that my instinct was to put it in a drawer
for six months and let the idea mature in my head before attempting
to have it published. John said that he himself was much interested in
the idea of how Jesus became thought of as divine, and would like to

put together a book of essays on this subject, of which my Samaritan proposal might be one. He had been talking to friends at Oxford, and felt there was enough interest in common to make such a book, with three contributors from Oxford and four from Birmingham, including himself, together with Don Cupitt, a radical from Cambridge. I agreed to consider this, and went to a meeting in Keble College, Oxford, where Dennis Nineham, who was Warden, hosted the occasion.

Nineham was sceptical about the whole project: having read the papers, he said that if he were asked to read the book for a publisher, he would recommend rejecting it. He saw value in John's own contribution, which maintained that the Incarnation was not a literal truth, but a myth or story designed to evoke suitable wonder from its hearers. He also liked Maurice Wiles' piece, which discussed meanings of the word 'myth'. But he thought little of the other Birmingham contributions; he called my theory a 'balon d'essai', which was not unfair; he thought nothing of an essay by Walter Hollenweger, an imaginative Swiss who was Professor of Mission at Birmingham. This was disappointing for Walter and embarrassing for us, but the oracle had spoken. The essayists met a number of times, and as my paper was novel and somewhat speculative, I did not resent the proposal to have an additional New Testament essay, by Frances Young. Fears were expressed that we should both seem too negative, and we were asked each to contribute a second, more positive piece. My second piece was better than the first; I said that Incarnation should be understood as meaning embodiment: Jesus was the embodiment of the love of God, in the same way that Churchill was the embodiment of British defiance in 1940. For a time we were still without a title for the book, but finally Frances came up with *The Myth of God Incarnate*, which was probably the most significant single contribution to our success.

John Bowden, the active publisher of SCM Press, accepted the book with alacrity, and launched it in 1977 with dramatic success. He engaged David Edwards, a popular theologian, to act as *Advocatus Dei*, and the occasion drew a large attendance from both the Press and the public. John avoided tricky questions like, 'Are you not then Unitarians?', with his customary skill: we were unitarians with a small 'u', but not with a capital 'U', which carried other overtones. David told an aggressive secularist questioner that he was just being rude. I was amazed by the impact which the book made, far beyond that of earlier liberal ventures. This was partly because Nineham and Wiles were members of an Archbishops' Commission on Doctrine. Within days there was a proposal in Synod that a vote of censure be passed on the essayists, and this was only avoided by Professor Lampe suggesting that it would be better not to take a vote until members had had a chance to read the book. But within weeks an evangelical counterblast had been published, *The Truth of God Incarnate*. The BBC wished to have a discussion of the book, but unluckily it had been published in July, and most of us had gone abroad, on holiday, or in my case to an SNTS Conference. This left Frances as our sole representative, and the programme consisted of an unedifying scene in which she was bullied by Michael Green and Stephen Neill. Green, with characteristic evangelical rhetoric, said, 'But if God did *not* get stuck in on the shop-floor, then the Christian Gospel is just fairy stories'. Frances had neither the character nor the wit to explain the difference between a myth and a fairy story, and allowed herself to be hectored into acknowledging that (in her view) the title had been a mistake. She was in any case a reluctant liberal; she wished to be part of a bold new theological endeavour, but she also wished to retain her influence in the rather conservative Methodist Church, of which she was a Minister.

The *Myth* was a *succès de scandale*, and sold forty thousand copies. But it increased my problems with what I believed. At first when I lectured for the Department I used to give courses on the Gospels or St Paul; but in time my classes would ask me to come again next year, and to tell them not what the evangelists thought, but what I thought myself. So I began to give courses entitled, 'Belief in God Today' in various centres around the West Midlands. These courses drew large audiences, and I ran them as cliff-hangers, moving week by week from Providence to Miracle to Prayer, and so on. People found this exciting as it forced them to question their own beliefs; but increasingly I began to feel bad as I was now unable to give a satisfactory answer to the questions I was raising, and I did not like playing games with people's fundamental creeds. In early 1981 I received a letter from Hong Kong. My old friend Canon Martin had died, and had left money to fund a Lectureship: would I like to come and give the Martin Lectures in the summer of that year? There would be two courses, one for the theological students and one for the general public. I accepted, suggesting as topics St Luke's Gospel and St Paul. At first this was agreed, but at the last minute the Committee wrote to say that they would rather have a more general subject for the public lectures. I could not easily say No at this juncture, so I said I would speak on 'Belief in God Today', the course I had tried out so successfully in England. I gave the lectures, but I found the experience traumatic. The public lectures were well attended and received with interest; but I felt increasingly the contradiction between what I was saying in this course and, on so frail a credal basis, to be encouraging young people in their training for the ministry. Matters came to a head with the question session after the last public lecture. My friend Philip Shen, a lecturer in Theology in the Chinese University, said, 'The critique [of Christian doctrine] has been very sharp, but the defence has been rather weak: how long do you think the Church can continue in this situation?' Philip later assured me that he meant the question exactly as posed, but at the time I felt it as questioning my sincerity—how long could *I* continue in this contradiction? Over the next weeks I began to feel that my integrity was involved, and the only proper thing was to take action and resign my Orders.

In the days when I was at Westcott House, I had been taught by Hugh Montefiore. He was now the Bishop of Birmingham, and about three years before this time I had been to consult him about my problems of faith; he had advised me to read his book on the subject, but unfortunately I had not found it convincing. I could not escape from the dilemma: it seemed impossible to think that God was providentially guiding all human affairs; but the alternative offered by John Hick was to believe in God because of our experience of Him, and I had had no such experience. At this point, on my return from Hong Kong, I received a postcard from Dennis Nineham, 'I understand that you are having doubts about your belief. You may like to know that I think that if you were to resign your Orders, almost everyone would approve'. I suspected that Dennis had been tipped the wink by Hugh, who was a friend of his; but I was grateful for the reassurance. I wrote to Hugh to resign my Orders as an Anglican priest in September 1981, and he was most understanding. I ceased being a clergyman without any fuss, and Dennis was right, that I faced very little criticism. In part I felt better, having taken what seemed to me an honourable course of action. But in another way I felt desolate. For thirty years the Church had been the centre of my life; I had preached its gospel, its saints had been my heroes, especially those whom I had known; its Year had been the pattern of my life, and I had said morning and evening prayer day by day. This structure of life was now gone, and those who had been my comrades in arms were that no more. I still loved the Church; Jesus and the Saints were still the patterns for my life; and I never wished to weaken anybody's faith, even though I no longer believed it myself. Since then it has had to be enough to follow the truth wherever it seemed to lead, and to try to live in charity with everyone.

Eighteen months later John Hick said to me, 'For fifteen years, Michael, you have spoken for the Christian faith in this City. Now that you have left the Church you owe it to those who have been your students to give an account of why you have made the change'. So we arranged a Saturday School in which from 11 a.m. to 4 p.m. we spoke alternately to the open-ended title, 'Why Believe in God?'. The hall was full, more than a hundred and fifty people, and it was a formidable occasion, since John was a professional philosopher and an excellent speaker; nonetheless I felt that, if anything, I got the better of the debate. John spoke first; he did not believe in the Providence of God, and his appeal therefore was restricted to claims of personal experience. He cited in particular Jesus' own experience of God; but Jesus clearly also had experiences of demons, in which John did not believe. He appealed also to experiences of God that had been collected by Alastair Hardy's Institute at Oxford; but although he could select one instance he found convincing, that of Leslie Weatherhead at Vauxhall Station, the book also contained a number of instances which did not at all accord with John's convictions. For example, one experience was that of a woman whose dog had died recently; she experienced seeing this dog looking up at a figure whom she took to be Jesus; but then John did not believe there were dogs in heaven either. Furthermore, we all often find that we have had experiences which do not quite accord with reality. I may go to a party and talk to a man whom I take to be charming; but later I find that he is a greasy fellow who was trying to get me to give him a job. John Baillie had spoken of his experience of God as Supreme Will and unconditional demand. But Ronald Hepburn contrasts such a claim with our more normal human experiences: 'We see the clenched fist and the tense facial muscles; we hear the full-throated command: this is the sergeant-major and no wraith'. It seems only too possible that Baillie's experience was his imagination. In my second talk I examined the widespread belief that we experience God in his Providential *action*. I took examples from the recent Falklands War, after which there had been services of thanksgiving for the victory. But I questioned what it was that God was supposed to have done, for which we were thanking Him. It was unclear whether it was that He had inspired our soldiers to greater bravery, or Mrs Thatcher to stiffer resolution, or whether He had intervened to divert or neutralize the Exocet missiles of the enemy. Another example of God's supposed action was the claim of the Catholic Cardinal after the election of Pope John Paul I, that they had elected 'God's Candidate'; but within six months the new Pope had died. We had asked John Bowden to be Chairman of the meeting, and afterwards he suggested that he publish the papers, with an autobiographical introduction by me, and a concluding chapter by John. This came out as a paperback, with the title *Why Believe in God?* later that year.

Chapter 15

THE BLACK AND WHITE CHRISTIAN PARTNERSHIP

While the *Myth* was in preparation, I became involved with a project which was to take much of my time over the next few years. Walter Hollenweger, the newly appointed Professor of Mission, was a Pentecostalist, and a scholar of the Pentecostal movement, in America, Africa and Britain. In the decade after the War many black people had come to Britain from the West Indies, often members of small independent churches. Walter had been to visit many of these, and had been impressed both by their quality and their weakness. Their pastors, who were often just the most facile speakers of the group, had no training and felt inferior to the white clergy whom they met, who often had degrees and theological books. Walter thought the University of Birmingham should provide a course for such people which would give them training and confidence, and he called together more than a hundred of them in 'A Small Beginning'; the pastors would not be internal students in the University, so the lectures would have to be provided by the Extramural Department, and would therefore be my responsibility. So I was included in the conference, and called upon to propose some practicable structure for the course. Walter wanted four courses in all, New Testament and Mission in the first year, Old Testament and Doctrine in the second. I saw that these would have to be weekend courses, with the pastors, coming as they did from all over the country, staying overnight in Birmingham. In this way they could have lectures on Friday night and through Saturday, with an Open Forum on Saturday evening, and worship in a variety of churches on Sunday.

Walter had founded a 'Centre for Black and White Christian Partnership' in the missionary colleges at Selly Oak, with a doctoral student of his as Director, a German pastorin called Roswith Gerloff. Roswith was a warm-hearted and practical person, though she was incorrigibly sentimental and painfully loquacious. She would be expected to find Christian families in the district who would be hosts to our students. Walter asked me to see him privately about the tutors. He said that

Roswith could be the tutor for the Mission course, and for the New Testament he said, 'I want the very best teaching that the University can provide...'. I thought, 'How generous of you, Walter'. Then he continued, '...so I thought we should invite Birdsall'. As Neville Birdsall was a pompous and prickly man I did not think it was a good choice, but I could hardly propose myself. I suggested to Neville that he go and meet Roswith, and plan the courses together; while she was teaching about Pentecostalism he could teach the New Testament doctrine of the Holy Spirit. The following Monday I received two letters, equally angry. Roswith wrote, 'Dr Birdsall seems to want to teach New Testament archaeology'; Neville wrote, 'Miss Gerloff seems to think that the blacks can teach us'. Both of these statements were pretty nearly true. Roswith did think that the blacks could teach us, a little humility at least. Neville withdrew for the moment, and when he finally did give a lecture he did not speak of Jesus or St Mark or St Paul but talked about Westcott and Hort and Molitor and Zunz. When he finished, the prophetess Fidelia rose from the ranks to announce that the Holy Spirit had not taken part in the lecture. Neville could not resist the Holy Spirit and at this point resigned finally. After this I had little alternative but to fill in as New Testament tutor, although I already had a full programme arranged of lectures elsewhere.

I attended the next weekend, and it could hardly have started more disastrously. Roswith had arranged for an opening lecture to be given by a well-known Selly Oak theologian, Lesslie Newbigin; she said this was part of the Mission course, but the lecture was on Romans 8. This was infuriating, as it was clearly trespassing into my area; but I need not have worried as the lecture was so bad. Newbigin spoke for nearly an hour, and even I was bored to tears. The experience was, however, a blessing in disguise: I realized at once that the pastors had a short attention span, and that lecturing was not open as a teaching method. I therefore moved over to teaching by dialogue. I would pick out one or two more confident members of the group, ask one of them to read a text aloud, and another to explain it. I would then lead a discussion on what the text really meant; I could often get sensible suggestions from the class, and was always appreciative. I wanted to get over the idea that Matthew the apostle could not have written the Gospel of Matthew, and after a while one Martin Simmonds said, 'Could it be that there were two people called Matthew—one the apostle and the other the evangelist?' I was so excited that I said, 'Blessed art thou, Martin bar-Simmonds; for flesh and blood hath not revealed this unto thee, but my Father in Heaven'. This teaching method was clearly popular and effective, and I soon found that it worked just as well with white middle-class students on other courses.

Newbigin's lecture was not the only trespass into my territory. Walter had written a play which he called 'Conflict in Corinth', and he had urged Roswith to get the students to produce it. This seemed a good idea since a shared project would help to build up a feeling of unity in the group. But Walter's play was an interpretation of Paul's First Letter to the Corinthians, and it was a highly tendentious interpretation. The NT text makes it clear that there were factions in the Corinthian church, and that some of the groups were richer than others. Walter was a semi-Marxist, and he thought that the apparently religious divisions really all boiled down to economic differences. This enabled him to encourage the black students to see themselves mirrored in the Bible, in a way that seemed to me quite unwarranted. But it was too late to stop the production of the play, which was already under way, and I was reduced to correcting the false impressions it created, an uphill struggle. Walter was a clever but unscrupulous man. I first became suspicious of him when I learned from his students that he would slice an onion into his handkerchief so as to enable him to weep visibly while recounting a moving episode during a lecture.

I sat in on the lecture he gave in Roswith's course. It was called 'The Three Types of Mission'. The first type was the Colonial type—example, David Livingstone. The attitude here is: 'We worship the true God, you worship idols; also we are civilized and you are savages; also we have guns and you have assegais'. The second type is the Monastic type—the Irish monks who settled among the Helvetii. They lived quietly among them, learning their language and writing it down. The third type is the Biblical type—example, Peter and Cornelius. Peter comes to Cornelius thinking to convert him, but learns instead from Cornelius that God views Gentiles as the equal of Jews. As soon as questions were invited, I said, 'One might think from your account that Paul was a Colonial missionary; he certainly believed that he was preaching the full truth, and that other religions were idolatry. Could you give us a second example, besides Peter with Cornelius, of the "Biblical" mission?' I got a lot of words back, but the short answer was there was no second example. The lecture was brilliant but unfairly slanted. Walter portrayed the great missionary movements of the nineteenth century as arrogant, contemptuous, racist ('savages'), and even violent. These missionary endeavours were viewed as the lowest of three steps of spirituality. The Irish monks, with their humble attention to their converts' culture, were a step more spiritual than David Livingstone; and the peak of spirituality was the so-called Biblical mission. This had a single example in the Bible, and the pastors were being encouraged to think of themselves as successors to Cornelius, who had something to teach their white English brethren. The misleading use of the term Biblical was intended to represent the incoming black churchmen as occupying the peak of spirituality. A year later I was surprised to find Walter giving the same lecture to the next intake of students; only this time the third type was not 'Biblical' but 'Dialogical', but the example offered of the last was still Cornelius. I again asked for a second example; and after some beating about the bush he suggested 'Vulfilas', who had evangelized the Goths, but in so doing had turned Jesus into a Gothic chieftain. However this was not at all like Cornelius, but a simple corruption of the Christian gospel.

The social side of the course also had its problems. Roswith persuaded local ministers and clergy to offer hospitality to our students for the weekend nights, and among church people who kindly responded was Josie Marsland, wife of the University's Vice-Chancellor. Professor Marsland was a charming and popular V.C., but he was not a believer himself. He had had polio in his youth, and was confined to a wheelchair. When Pastor Taiwo entered the house he saw in a moment that he could repay his hosts for their kindness. He announced that he would pray for the Professor, laying hands on his head, and that he would be healed. Marsland said courteously that he was not a Christian and would much prefer not to be prayed over; but Taiwo assured him that faith was not required, and that Jesus' prayers were always answered in the healing of sufferers. So he went ahead, laid his hands on Marsland's head, and prayed; but nothing happened. The following morning Marsland suggested to his wife that they should not have Taiwo again. But when the Centre tried to inform Taiwo, it was discovered that he had been arrested as an illegal immigrant. He had come from Ghana and jumped ship at Southampton, and was now sent to Pentonville until he should be deported. One of the Selly Oak staff went to visit him in prison and found him quite happy, having made many converts among his fellow convicts.

The Sunday worship was often the most educative part of the weekend. The first time we went to the church of the Cherubim and Seraphim. We were warned in advance that God had said to Moses, 'Take off thy shoes from off thy feet, for the place whereon thou standest is holy ground', and that the same rule applied in this church. On arrival I took off my shoes and handed them to a waiting church member to be stored with those of the others; however, when it was realized that I was a lecturer on the course, my shoes were at once whisked off to be stored with those of other VIPs somewhere in the back. I had brought a student with me in the car and he asked if I would give him a lift to the station to catch the 12.30 to London; as it was 10.00 I thought this could be managed without difficulty. However we did not begin punctually and the programme provided indicated a varied series of elements; no.6 of these was marked 'Visions (if any)', and as time advanced I realized that we would only make the train if there were no visions. But in fact there was no shortage of visionaries; both prophetesses and prophets revealed what the Angel had told them in the prayer-time; there would be a hard winter, a miners' strike, and other troubles. When the visions were finished, it was time for me to go, but the next item was a dance, and I found it impossible to get through and recover my shoes. We eventually secured them, but were held up at the door by a kind Secretary of the church who pressed us to eat some cake. I am afraid my friend missed his train.

A regular feature of black services was an initial Sunday School, usually taught by a large matron, and dependent on an American textbook. Some of these teachings horrified the white members of our course. They were asked what Eve should have done when tempted by the serpent, and the answer supplied was, 'She should have asked her husband'. This was not acceptable to a mildly feminist Canadian on the course, and the teacher found herself embroiled in an emotional topic. This turned out to be fruitful, for it raised the question of the authority of Scripture, and this was soon extended to the justification of slavery, for which St Paul could be cited. I felt that the mixture of the races on the course was being helpful to both sides.

For variety of worship we cast our net wide, including even the Coptic church in Hampton-in-Arden; this meant an early start, for their service began at 8.30 a.m., and we had to get there. They were accommodating, in that they abbreviated the service to four hours, and the lessons and sermon were in English. I knew no Coptic, but could make out various phrases in Greek. After the service we were welcomed to refreshments, which consisted of a vegetarian sandwich, as it was Lent. To my surprise the hall was full of regular worshippers, almost all Egyptian doctors who had come from all corners of the kingdom. One of these doctors engaged me in conversation, deploring the failure of British churches to believe in miracles; I asked if he had ever witnessed a miracle, and he said that he had indeed. He had been trained in Cairo, and when the list had gone up of the students' vivas, he found that he was to be examined by a professor who always failed all Christian students on principle. He had prayed to the Virgin, and when he turned up the next morning his examiner had been changed to a more liberal person.

Other visits were educational in a less edifying way. Father Foley, a charming Catholic priest, was attending our course, and invited us to his church. I was anxious that the blacks might be scandalized by prayer to the Virgin Mary, but it was not this which offended them, but the sheet of church notices. Most black churches are puritan; they do not smoke or drink or gamble or go to cinemas. But here the notices ran, 'Monday: Bingo...Tuesday: the Parish Draw...Wednesday: Mega-Bucks...'. To our students the Holy Catholic Church appeared to be a den of vice, inviting its unhappy members down the path to ruin in this life, and worse beyond.

Our experience of the Church of England was, if anything, worse. Roswith went to see John Waterstreet, the Vicar of St Mary's, Selly Oak; he was happy to welcome us, but displayed nervousness about our willingness to fit in with the church timetable. He would be content for one of our pastors to preach, but only for twenty minutes. From our point of view the service was a disaster. Black services have the great merit of being joyful, and nothing could be less joyful than Anglican Mattins with the Venite and a psalm chanted, and then the Te Deum recited. It so happened that that Sunday there was a bus strike, and in consequence our students arrived in the middle of the service, carrying their electric guitars. Our preacher was not used to having his time limited, and was nervous and uncomfortable; black preachers are used to supporting cries from the congregation of 'Hallelujah', and 'Ay-men'; but Anglicans are not used to this, and the sermon was greeted in silence. John Waterstreet closed the service in a hurry with a Blessing, to enable his flock to go home to lunch, while our students joined together in prayer and song accompanied by the guitars.

Despite these misadventures, the Black and White course was in general a success. Each weekend we had between thirty and forty students, about a third of them white. The different races got on well, and friendships soon developed. The white students appreciated the vitality of black religion; they joined with spirit in the singing of choruses, and enjoyed the element of responsiveness in a black service. The Saturday evening Forums were often successful. We had, for instance, a lively debate between a white hospital chaplain and John Adigoke, a firm believer in the power of prayer to heal. Hollenweger himself thought that most healings in black services would have happened naturally, but John was adamant that Jesus had said, 'Heal the sick', and in a service in his church he laid hands on a sick person and told the congregation, 'He will be healed'. The fame of the course extended to the Continent; we received substantial subsidies from both Switzerland and Germany, and two ministers' daughters came from Germany to work with the Centre for six months without charge. One weekend we had a deputation of some twenty Germans who sat in on our sessions. The first of these was unfortunate. Roswith had invited a sociologist to explain the dynamics of a society, and he took as his example the Steam Train Association, of which he was a member. The lecture passed over the heads of our students, and to give him an opportunity to explain its relevance, I asked what was the difference between the Steam Train Association and the Church of God. The speaker had been demoralized by the evident failure of his talk, and could not answer fluently; however one of our German visitors stepped in helpfully to fill the gap: 'I will tell you the difference. The Church of God is an *eschatological* society'. Happily the New Testament session went smoothly, and the Germans were delighted by what they called 'a merry Bible study'.

I had resigned my Orders in September 1981, and the next term began a few days later. I was relieved when Roswith suggested telling this to the students, and asking them if they were happy for me to go on teaching them. It was touching to hear one after another saying how much they had enjoyed my course and learned from it; and the matter was summed up by Deacon Barrett, not the brightest member of the course, who said, 'It is his calling to teach us, and it is our calling to convert him; and we shall do so, for it is written, "He will have mercy on whom He will have mercy"'. The kindly prophet had forgotten the second half of the verse, '...and whom He will, he hardeneth'. It was heartening that, despite (or because of) their strong faith, they were prepared to allow a non-believer to teach them.

The end of the year brought the dreaded examinations. As I ran each lecture as a dialogue, it was impossible for the students to take notes, and I had supplied them with a typed copy of the outline of each lecture. I advised them to prepare for the exams by revising these lecture sheets carefully, and the result was reassuring. When I marked the papers a pleasing proportion of the students had passed, and some at a very high standard; to one of them I gave 85%. When I boasted of this to Carolyn Hick, my psychologist colleague, she asked, with unnerving percipience, 'Was she pretty, Michael?' The arrow was near the mark, for there was only one student on the course who could have produced answers of such quality, and that was Kathryn, my Canadian student from Saskatchewan; and she was not so much pretty as beautiful. However this significant fact was unknown to the Theology Department lecturers who double-marked the papers, and confirmed the grades which I had given. Double-marking external students' exam papers is a chore, but Iain Torrance, the senior

New Testament lecturer, wrote to me, 'I enjoyed marking your students' papers, and learned from them'. So generous a compliment might be unique. We had a farewell celebration after this, and I was able to say to the students, 'I have done my half of the bargain' [to teach them], 'but I'm afraid you have not managed to do yours'.

Chapter 16

The Path to Recognition

My Speaker's Lectures on Matthew's Gospel were published in 1974, and received a long and favourable review, written by Anthony Harvey in the *Journal of Theological Studies*. Austin had earlier advised that I should apply for a D.D. (Doctor of Divinity, which is the highest degree that Oxford confers), and the University regulations specified that I should submit published material to support the application. This was now available in the form of *Midrash and Lection in Matthew*, and I accordingly put in my application. The University Theology Faculty appointed three judges to consider the work: Geoffrey Lampe, Professor at Cambridge, Barnabas Lindars, Professor at Manchester, and Anthony Harvey, an Oxford scholar who had distinguished himself with a Commentary on the New English Bible. The three were not united: Lampe was inclined to accept it, Barnabas to refuse it. Anthony wrote to the others, saying, 'If Goulder had written a dull book with as much learning as this, we should have given him the Doctorate. Why should we refuse it when he has written an interesting book?' So Anthony prevailed, and I became a D.D. I was invited to lunch at Trinity, my old college, before the ceremony in the Sheldonian, and we drove down to stay with my mother the night before. We left Wingfield in two cars, Clare driving the girls and my mother taking me in her Sunbeam Talbot. She chose the familiar but winding A423 road via Henley-on-Thames, and soon we found ourselves behind a large vehicle bearing the notice 'Steam Traction Engine No. 60'; when the road was straight enough we had the speed to pass this thing, only to find ourselves behind a similar monster marked 'Steam Traction Engine No. 59'. We had happened to coincide with a rally of these vehicles, and had in time to pass all sixty of them. This put our lunch in peril, but we arrived with a few minutes to spare, and I was able to take my place at the head of the procession into the Sheldonian with due solemnity. The D.D. has a splendid scarlet hood as its symbol, and this together with the prestige which the Doctorate carries enabled me to feel that I had in some sense arrived as a scholar.

In other ways recognition came slowly. Neirynck's period as Chairman of the SNTS Synoptic Seminar came to an end, and Bernard Orchard proposed me as his successor; at the time I was surprised to have arrived so soon at such an influential position, but in fact I was the only obvious candidate. For the following year I invited Christopher Tuckett, a young British scholar from Manchester, to give a paper on the Beatitudes, and this was a considerable success. It is often claimed that Luke's form of the Beatitudes is earlier than Matthew's, and represents the Q form; this would be a strong argument against Farrer's theory, and I was keen therefore to disprove it. The situation was a little tricky, as I was both the Chairman and the principal interlocutor; on the whole I got the better of the argument, and the two positions were published together later. A new member had joined the Seminar, a leading American called James Robinson; I spoke to him as I left the meeting, and was surprised that he said to me, 'Of course this kind of argument is your *forte*'. The comment took me aback, not just because he pronounced the word as 'fort' but because arguments from the usages preferred by Luke and Matthew are fundamental to the discussion, and are not anybody's special strong point.

Robinson was a character, not always an easy one; he was something found in America but rare in Europe, an entrepreneur scholar. The SNTS had been founded in the 1930s as an Anglo-European venture, and after the War the practice was resumed of holding the meetings alternately in Britain and on the Continent. This fretted American scholars, who wished some meetings to be held in the New World, and in 1971 Robinson announced that he had arranged for a chartered plane to bring 167 members of the Society to Claremont in California the following year; the trip would be free from Heathrow to Claremont, all expenses found, including hotel and conference costs. This generous offer was gratefully accepted, despite some German hesitation as to whether it was religiously responsible to put so many New Testament eggs (eggheads?) in one basket. The Conference was not an undiluted success, however; the tensions were too much for James' volatile temperament, and at one stage he and the Committee had semi-public disagreements.

About this time some significant documents which had been dis-covered in the sands of Upper Egypt in 1945 were at length published, through the enterprise of James Robinson; these were Gnostic texts, the Nag Hammadi texts, mostly from one or two centuries after the New Testament, but very interesting for seeing how Christianity had developed. Middle Eastern traders soon scented that these texts were worth money and they began to change hands in black markets over the area. James realized their significance, and raised sufficient funds to pursue them and buy everything he could lay hands on. They were then transferred to California, where he translated them and published them for scholarly use. For a third entrepreneurial venture he founded an institute at Claremont for the study of the hypothetical document Q. He organized a considerable staff of post-graduate students, and a large community of international scholars, and began publishing a series of volumes on Q; each volume discussed a few verses of the supposed text, gathering and citing the opinions of all scholars who had published on them over the last two hundred years. This enormous endeavour was called the IQP, or International Q Project, and became an important element in subsequent discussion. It had originated as a consultation in the Society of Biblical Literature, but developed into an independent enterprise. There still is a Q Seminar in the SBL, but it has diminished to a shadow of its former self, and the speakers today are often Q-sceptics, and followers of the Farrer Theory.

In 1979, the year after I had hosted the British NT Conference in Birmingham, the Conference was held in Edinburgh, and I was invited to give the opening paper. I did this as a trenchant attack on Q, calling it 'A House Built on Sand'. I described the original error on which Q had been based in the 1800s, and various additional contradictions in which it was mired. The paper went down well, and I was pleased that a number of competent defenders of Q were present, who tried in vain to dispute with me. Foremost among these was Christopher Tuckett, whom I had encouraged when I invited him to speak at the SNTS Seminar in 1978. We crossed swords at a series of further conferences, organized by Bernard Orchard and held mostly at Ampleforth Abbey in Yorkshire. Here I found that I had a number of useful allies: John Drury, who had been an enthusiastic follower of my Speaker's Lectures at Oxford, John Fenton, a senior Oxford lecturer, and Benedict Green, once a fellow scholar with me at Eton, and now an Anglican monk at Mirfield.

After so many months of defending Farrer's theory *contra mundum*, it was encouraging to find that I had the support of a ring of friendly faces at this conference. But far more encouraging was the endorsement of Ed Sanders, Dean Ireland Professor of NT at Oxford, who discussed the problem in *Studying the Synoptic Gospels*, written with Margaret Davies, 1989, and concluded that my solution was substantially correct. It would be hard to exaggerate the value of this comment. Sanders was one of the two or three leading NT critics in the world, and he shows here a marked shift from his position in the 1960s, when he had inclined to support Farmer. The book is still in print and widely read by many students of the Gospels, and is cited in every introduction. This was the great step forward for my theory.

The last of Bernard Orchard's conferences was held at Göttingen in 1991, and was restricted to 'The Minor Agreements'. There were a dozen or so leading scholars invited to this, with Georg Strecker as host. The opening paper was by Neirynck, and the leading disputant was Albert Fuchs, an Austrian whose habitual intransigence made him a difficult colleague. He was sufficiently unwilling to concede an inch to Neirynck that the latter became impatient; Strecker called the meeting to move on, and Neirynck slammed his book shut, and looked as if he would walk out of the room. Luckily for me Strecker called for more questions, and I was able to make three telling points. Over lunch with another Austrian scholar called Niemand, I remarked that we had seen a bit of emotion. Niemand replied, 'But there is a difference between the two men: Neirynck would die for his hypothesis; Fuchs would kill for his'. My thought went back to Virgil: 'Tantaene animis caelestibus irae?'

In the afternoon I had my slot, and I had given it to my old favourite text, 'Who is it who smote thee?' which I had raised at Birmingham years before. Neirynck and Tuckett both supported Streeter's line, that all the manuscripts of Matthew had been corrupted. This always seemed to me grossly implausible, and I recounted in my paper a conversation I had had in Milan with Barbara Aland, the leading NT textual scholar. I had asked her, 'What would you think of a widely held NT theory which depended on the idea that all the manuscripts had been corrupted?' She replied, 'Of course such a theory would be absurd; but what theory are you thinking of?' I said, 'The Q theory', citing the present passage. I told this anecdote without giving Barbara's name, but when I referred to her as 'she', her identity became obvious. As the proceedings were to be published, Neirynck was unwilling to have his weak position exposed in this way, and he wrote to Professor Aland asking her to modify her opposition. So in due course I received a letter from her apologising for having spoken too hastily, and asking me to withdraw the reference to our Milan discussion.

During the 1980s my friend John Hick was part-time Professor at Claremont Graduate School in California. While there, he was consulted about inviting a European scholar to give an Old Testament lecture bequeathed in the names of two honoured teachers called Knopf and Hill, and he recommended me. I was invited with expenses paid one way, and was able to get myself an invitation to give further lectures in Pennsylvania to pay my flight home. I gave my lecture on Psalm 68, which was well received, and I enjoyed staying with the Hicks in their comfortable home. As I was on the spot, James Robinson took the opportunity of asking me to read a paper to his Q seminar, which I was pleased to do. James and his wife asked me to dinner first, and we then proceeded to the Seminar room. There were about twenty of his post-graduates present, and I gave them the same critique of Q as that which had gone down well at Edinburgh, 'A House Built on Sand'. To my surprise, James chaired the meeting, but at no point took part in the discussion. His students asked some innocuous questions, and several times commented that I had not referred to Secret Mark, a document valued in America but in Europe believed (and later proved) to be a forgery. John remarked that the evening had been not so much a success as a triumph; and the next day one of those present said to me that this was the first time James had been silent at such a meeting. It was remarkable that James should have been fully aware of my work on the Synoptic Problem, and yet have virtually ignored it in the IQP publications. Naturally this drew criticism, and but for the steady work of Kloppenborg would have cost the IQP most of its reputation.

I began to feel that he had not asked me in order to have a proper discussion but as an exercise for his students to cut their teeth on. With the Göttingen experience and Barbara Alend's letter to follow, I was increasingly aware that the water was not flowing in my direction. I was making excellent points and they were not being attended to. The multiplication of Q volumes produced by James' Institute was in itself a guarantee that Q was securely based in people's minds despite my efforts to shake it. I needed a new argument, and at this stage one occurred to me. Matthew has a more stereotyped style than Luke, with certain favourite phrases which recur often. When Matthew and Luke differ slightly in Q passages, it is often found that Matthew's wording includes some regular expression of his; the Standard Hypothesis then tends to credit the Lucan form as 'the original Q form', because it can then explain the Matthaean variant as due to Matthew's substitution of his favoured expression. We make take as an example the Lord's Prayer, which I have set out above on page 36. The Standard Hypothesis supposes that the Lucan form is that which stood in Q, because it can then explain Matthew's 'Our Father in heaven' as due to Matthew's liking for this expression, which comes 32 times in his Gospel, only once in Mark and not at all in Luke. Of course this involves assuming that Q had a different style from Matthew's, as otherwise 'Our Father in heaven' would have to be ascribed to Q. However, this assumption then leads on to a difficulty: Luke's wording and Matthew's in many Q passages are in close, even verbatim agreement; and these passages often include others of Matthew's favourite phrases, for example, 'You offspring of vipers', 'O ye of little faith', 'There shall be weeping and gnashing of teeth', and a dozen more. Since these phrases come also in non-Q parts in Matthew, the question must arise how this can be so. The natural defence is that Matthew and Q had very similar styles, and that Matthew took such phrases over from Q. But then, when Luke and Matthew differed in the wording of Q material, as in the Lord's Prayer, it was assumed that Q's style was *different* from Matthew's. We shall not get nearer the truth with a hypothesis which involves self-contradiction. Rather, one is driven to suppose that Matthew and Q were the same person; or, to speak more simply, the whole Q theory is unnecessary. We should accept that Matthew composed the so-called Q material, just as he composed the rest of his Gospel, using his own preferred phrasing. As Farrer said, Luke was familiar with Matthew's Gospel and took over those passages which he found most attractive, sometimes slightly varying the phrasing and sometimes writing it out word for word. I explained this argument in two articles in *The Journal of Biblical Literature*, 'Is Q a Juggernaut?' and 'Self-Contradiction in the IQP'.

I had opportunity to try out my new theory at two main papers at the SNTS which were expositions of Q; I had given up the hope that Neirynck would recant the Q hypothesis in print, but the next best thing was publicly to embarrass its defenders. One of these papers was by Professor Howard Kee, an American, whose topic was the Q text, 'They say a glutton and a wine-bibber'. This was convenient for me because the Greek has, 'A glutton and a wine-bibber *man*', and this use of *anthropos* with a noun is found elsewhere in Matthew, 'a king-man', 'a householder-man'; and in Matthew only. I was able to give the Greek for all these passages, and to ask if he agreed with me that Q scholars were trying to have it both ways, taking Q's style to be similar to Matthew's when it suited them and dissimilar when it did not. Professor Kee did not agree with me, as I knew he wouldn't, but he could not offer an explanation for these facts and was visibly embarrassed. A similar situation arose two years later when a German scholar took a Q text as his subject. I made the same objection as I had made to Kee, and again there was no answer to it, but this time it was less effective because the speaker's understanding of English was not good enough to follow the argument.

For many years I was too diffident, and too sensible, to raise my voice at SNTS Main Papers; but in time I came to feel quite at ease on my feet. At the Chicago meeting of the Society in 1986 Jimmy Dunn, one of the most respected of British scholars, gave a Main Paper. Jimmy believed that the Gospels preserved Jesus' teachings, almost undiluted, and he took as an example of this comfortable doctrine the discussion of food-laws in Mark ch.7. Here Jesus is portrayed as a liberal: it is not what goes into a man which defiles him, but the evil thoughts which come out of him. Mark explains that he said this, declaring all food clean. It so happens that Paul discusses the same issue in Romans ch.14, and takes the same line, remarking that 'Nothing is unclean of itself'. Jimmy argued that Paul was familiar with Jesus' teaching as preserved in Mark; but this argument seemed to me extremely weak. I tried to catch the President's eye, but he did not notice me, perhaps preferring more eminent questioners. The President was Martin Hengel, and by chance his wife was sitting next to me, and she was kind enough to draw his attention to me. There was, as I said, another possibility of relating the two texts: Paul was anxious that Jewish food laws should not be imposed on his Gentile converts, and it might well be that Mark, who was an associate of Paul's, placed this teaching in Jesus' mouth. The trouble from Jimmy's point of view was the debate on the same topic between Peter and Paul in Galatians ch.2; here it is Paul who is the liberal and Peter the conservative. This allowed me to move in for the kill. I asked, 'Do you think that Peter was not paying attention when Jesus explained the matter?...Or do you think that Jesus was in rather a muddle, and took one position at one time and one at another?' These questions were greeted by two roars of sustained laughter round the hall. Jimmy replied, 'That is a typical Michael Goulder question'; but it was one he could not answer. After this I did not again find any difficulty in attracting the President's attention.

With such successes at the SNTS and a lengthening list of published articles, I began to feel that a scholar is not without honour save in his own University. There were two New Testament Professors in the Theology Department, Neville Birdsall and Frances Young, and I felt that I was abler than both of them. Neville was a manuscript expert with no great interest in the NT itself; Frances was a Patristic scholar whose NT theories I found unconvincing. Rob Sawers, the Director of the Extramural Department, proposed me for a Chair, and the Theology Department accepted the idea; but the VC referred the matter to Gordon Davies, the retired Professor of Theology, and he vetoed it. However, I had an influential friend in John Hull, the blind Professor of Religious Education, who was now Dean of the Faculty. He renewed the application, with the support of Jennifer Tann, our new Director, this time with success. But the VC delayed it this time too, by referring the matter to the Bishop of Birmingham, whose relevance did not seem obvious to me, since an academic post should not be dependent on one's faith but on one's scholarship; however, he made no objection. So, at last, in 1991, at the age of sixty-four, I became Professor of Biblical Studies, and delivered my Inaugural Lecture some fifteen months later.

After such a long wait this proved to be a most heart-warming occasion. New Professors commonly read their Inaugurals from prepared texts, but John Hull, being blind, had just delivered his Inaugural Lecture, very successfully, speaking from memory; so I thought that, with my experience of giving public lectures, I would take the risk and just talk naturally. The Lecture was held in the Education Department building; the hall was steeply tiered, and every seat was taken, even the gallery, with people sitting (illegally) on the stairs. Those who had been to my lectures in different places attended in good numbers. I went in early, to put out some handouts, and a busload of my students from Tettenhall came in at the back as I was doing this. I could not get past them, so I welcomed them each by name as they came in, and a visiting Professor remarked approvingly that he had never seen this done before. When the proceedings started there were about 400 people in the hall (far more than is usual at such occasions), and they included a good sprinkling of my black pastors, who came loyally on the encouragement of Patrick Kalilombe, Roswith Gerloff's successor. People were heard saying, 'What are all these black people doing here?'—which was precisely what Patrick had intended; he wanted to show that this was their University too. The Pro-Vice-Chancellor introduced me, commenting that he had never seen such a queue of cars for an Inaugural, and that you could not park for half a mile! As soon as I began speaking, I felt the warmth of the response; I was pleased to be free just to talk, and cracked my jokes easily.

I had developed a unitary theory to account for numerous details in the NT, and this gave the lecture a simple narrative structure. I called it 'A Tale of Two Missions': Paul says in Galatians ch.2 that the mission to the Gentiles was entrusted to him, in the same way that the mission to the Jews was entrusted to Peter. The context reveals that the two missions were already at loggerheads. The documents of the New Testament were written in Greek, which was the language of the Pauline mission, and this suggests that they were written by members of the Pauline movement. The numerous tensions revealed in these documents should be explained in the light of the struggle between the two movements. For instance, Mark says that Jesus' mother and brothers tried to interrupt his preaching, and that Jesus said that those who harkened to his preaching were his real mother and brothers; this corresponds to the fact that the Jerusalem church, by now headed by Jesus' brother James, had tried to interfere with the Pauline mission. The Jerusalem church had originally been founded by Peter and James and John, the sons of Zebedee; so Mark takes a very unsympathetic view of these men in the second half of his Gospel. Peter is portrayed as not understanding Jesus' statement that he must suffer; James and John tried to claim the best seats in the Kingdom of God; all three of them went to sleep instead of praying in Gethsemane, and Peter ended by denying Jesus three times. All this is Mark's attempt to diminish the authority of the Jerusalem mission, whose converts at Corinth proclaimed their allegiance to Peter, saying, 'I am of Cephas' (i.e. Peter).

At first the battle was over whether Gentile converts should have to keep Jewish rules: hence Mark's insistence that Jesus said that all food is clean, and that the Sabbath was made for man and not man for the Sabbath. But in time the issue extended to the more fundamental matter of Christology, that is, the question of who Jesus was. In his lifetime disciples had addressed him as 'Lord', a normal title of honour; and Jesus had compared his dying and returning to the lord of a household's going away for the evening. Many Jewish people expected the Messiah to come during the night of the Feast of Passover, and a year after Jesus' death the Jerusalem church was praying, '*Marana tha*'—that is, 'Our Lord, come'. This use of the word Lord was to be of critical importance: the Greek translation of the Old Testament, the Septuagint, regularly uses the word as a translation for the divine name Yahweh; and this led Pauline Christians, with their Greek bibles, to understand Jesus as a divine Lord. Paul thought of him as an eternal being alongside God in Heaven, who became a man at his conception. However, this kind of interpretation seemed to Jewish Christians to be blasphemous; to them Jesus had been a normal human being, of exceptional virtue and wisdom, on whom God had sent a divine spirit at his Baptism. This vital division between the two missions is reflected in John's Gospel. We hear that Jesus' brothers did not believe in him, and that 'those Jews who had believed in him' were offended by Jesus' claim that God was his Father, and that they took up stones to stone him for his blasphemy. It is John who tells us that before he became a man Jesus was the 'Word', that is, an extension of God, and that the Word became flesh; this is a full statement of the Incarnation doctrine already taught in outline by Paul. With Jewish Christians giving central importance to Jesus' Baptism, John totally omits the event. In his Letters, he becomes more openly combative: 'Many false prophets have gone out into the world' (he means from Jerusalem); their error consists in that 'they do not acknowledge Jesus'; it is likely that they did acknowledge the divine spirit which had possessed Jesus, but they would not confess the human Jesus to be divine as that would be blasphemy. John insists that he preached Jesus Christ 'come in the flesh'. He stresses, 'He came not through water only' (that is, not in the Baptism), '...but through water and blood'. Jewish biology believed that humanity was a compound of blood and water: 'There are three that bear witness, the spirit and the water and the blood; and these three combine in one unity'; John brings this out with much emphasis in his description of Jesus' death. When he died, he did not just give up the spirit, he 'handed it over' to God. The soldier then pierces his side, and there come out water and blood. John gives the greatest possible stress to this by adding that the Beloved Disciple saw it and has borne witness to it. In other words we have his guarantee that Jesus Christ was totally human, spirit, water and blood.

I had to infer the opinions of Jewish Christians from their main opponent, St John; but in the second century Irenaeus tells us of some Jewish Christians, Ebionites; and the Fathers give us extensive quotations from the Ebionite Gospel. The name comes from the Hebrew *ebyonim*, poor people; because, on their own account, they had shared their money between them. They thought Jesus was a normal human being, the son of Mary and Joseph, conceived in the usual way; but that he was better than other men, and at his Baptism the heavenly powers sent 'Christ', a divine spirit, to take him over, so that he was able to perform miracles and teach about the Unknown Father. Spirits cannot suffer, so before his Passion 'Christ' left Jesus, who then died and rose again. Thus in these documents we have full evidence of the Christology of those Jewish Christians.

The lecture was a great success. I was nervous that it was too long and abbreviated the last part; but this was a mistake, for many people came and asked me about it afterwards. The University used to issue invitations to Inaugural Lectures, pink invitations which included refreshments afterwards for the select, white ones for the rest. But John Hull, the Dean, did not approve of University parsimony, and had the tables set out in the hall behind the lecture room, with wine for all. Naturally the *hoi polloi* with white cards did not know that they had not been invited, and helped themselves along with the others; the manager came to John to say the wine was running out, and John said, 'Go to Professor Goulder, and ask him what happened at Cana of Galilee'.

An hour was sufficient to set out the outline of my Two Missions theory; and I was able soon afterwards to publish a revised version under the same title, *A Tale of Two Missions*. But in the meantime it had occurred to me that the same theory would explain many of the problematic NT texts, and I published a number of articles in the 90's expounding this (whose details can be found in the bibliography to the present book). The opposition at Corinth, for example, were Jewish Christians ('*Sophia in I Corinthians*', 'Vision and Knowledge'); and the same was true of the opposition in other towns ('Silas in Thessalonica', 'The Visionaries of Laodicea'). The same, moreover, was true of the opposition being criticized in Mark's Gospel ('Those Outside', 'A Pauline in a Jacobite Church'); and the same principle applies to the Pastoral Epistles ('The Pastor's Wolves'), and on to the Jewish Christian community known as the Ebionites in the second century ('A Poor Man's Christology'). The opposition at Corinth was a cardinal point in my theory. This was partly because the two Corinthian Epistles are so large a proportion of the Pauline letters; and we should expect to find evidence of a Jewish-Christian opposition somewhere here. Also, many scholars believed, erroneously, that the Corinthian opposition followed a leader called Apollos. I developed the argument against this into a book, *Paul and the Competing Mission at Corinth*, which was published in America and was well reviewed by Douglas Campbell.

Three years later the SNTS Conference was held at Edinburgh, where my friend John O'Neill was Professor. On the Tuesday there was a *ceilidh*, a Scottish celebration with whisky and dancing, during which John announced that there would be two presentations. One was to a Scottish scholar, and to my amazement I heard that the other one was for me. This was a *Festschrift*. It is quite common, when a scholar approaches retirement, for his doctoral students to put together a book of essays in his honour. But, teaching in the Extramural Department, I had had no doctoral students; so I had never thought such an honour would come my way. My friend Paul Joyce, an Old Testament scholar whom I had been surprised to see at the occasion, had joined with two NT scholars, Stanley Porter and David Orton, to put together this *Festschrift* for me. They had given the book the felicitous title *Crossing the Boundaries*, a double reference to my work in both Testaments, and also to my having left the Church—there was also an echo of my interest in cricket. It was a wonderful moment, and I was moved and gratified by the widespread applause which greeted the announcement.

A *Festschrift* was an excitement; but even more exciting was the arrival in my life of Mark Goodacre. I mentioned above my debate with John Hick as part of a series of public disputations. These were held on Saturdays from 11.00 a.m. to 4.00 p.m., with an hour's break for lunch. I used to organize six of these each year, normally three on a doctrinal topic, and three on a biblical one. The programme thus looked varied:

'Is Christianity the True Religion?', 'Did Jesus Rise from the Dead?'; but more workaday titles, like 'Isaiah' or 'The Pastoral Epistles' would also draw three-figure audiences. With such a public it was possible to attract some of the best-known speakers in the country, such as Don Cupitt, Rowan Williams, Gabriel Josipovici, Hugh Montefiore, Hermann Bondi, and Ed Sanders. Many of those who attended came regularly, RE teachers, clergy, lay readers, etc. Usually I took the chair myself, though sometimes I thought it would go better if I were one of the disputants. The success of the series depended in part on my supplying an element of novelty and imagination, while scholars like Frances Young or David Catchpole could defend more orthodox positions. It was also a help that I made no secret of my wish to entertain as well as to instruct, and the days were usually felt to be very enjoyable.

Among those who came was an RE teacher called Janet Goodacre, from Burton-on-Trent; and I noticed that once or twice she brought a bright-looking bespectacled fifteen-year-old with her. After a while I was visiting Oxford, and my colleague John Day, a don at Lady Margaret Hall, remarked to me, 'One of your students has been offered a scholarship here'. I was puzzled, as I did not have any schoolboy students, but John said, 'Well, his papers were full of your theories'. I guessed at once that this must be Janet's son, and so it was. Mark actually went to Exeter College, and three years later he gained the top First of his year. I had a letter from him soon afterwards saying that he was hoping to write a DPhil thesis on my work, and could he come up and discuss it with me? It was only now that I began to realize that Mark was pure, 24-carat, gold: he had a sharp power of observation, a lively imagination, and good judgement, and this combination of gifts is not common among scholars. He was also a delightful person. He wrote the thesis under the supervision of John Muddiman, a one-time pupil of Austin Farrer, and it was published under the title *Goulder and the Gospels*. The book delighted me, for it combined a general approval of my four principal theories with some sharp detailed criticism. He was able to think up tests for matters like my Lectionary hypothesis, and to notice weak points in the theory; I think he endorsed rather more than about three out of four of my theories, but the book gained a lot by its not being of merely uncritical approbation.

Scholars achieve recognition in large measure by attracting younger students who can develop their ideas; and with Mark's arrival in my life a most important threshold had been crossed. These were not Mark's only assets. He became also a wizard with a computer, and produced a series of websites which were visited by thousands. His 'NT Gateway' provided an introduction to different NT topics, with extensive reading lists, and this was used not only by numerous students beginning their studies, but also by established scholars across two continents. Later he regarded this as an important means of overthrowing established critical positions: when I began NT study, I read Streeter's standard *The Four Gospels*, and accepted the general view that this represented the established truth; but modern students do not only read such works, but surf the net and find, printed out on Mark's website, articles by Austin Farrer, Goulder, and Goodacre himself, all arguing that Streeter was wrong, and presenting Farrer's theory instead.

So Mark became a Doctor of Philosophy at Oxford, a high achievement; but such achievements carry no money with them, nor any guarantee of an academic job. With a wife and a small daughter to feed he soon found himself employed at Disney World, where for £3.60 an hour he welcomed the customers, saw they did not filch the goods, and scraped the chewing-gum off the carpet when they had left. It was months before his luck turned. Frances Young, Professor of Theology at Birmingham, was promoted to be Pro-Vice-Chancellor, and this created the need for a Tutor in New Testament and Patristics. I heard about the vacancy three days before the closing date, and Mark was just in time to apply. He sparkled at the interview, and to my delight was given the job; thus for some years he worked in Birmingham, and we could see plenty of each other. He was a most successful teacher, partly because he explained things clearly and attractively, and partly because he put his foot down on discipline; if the students had not done the preparatory work for a seminar, there was no seminar. Such firmness is risky, for the students might call his bluff by repeatedly not doing the work, but Mark held his nerve and was successful.

Although the new work required much preparation, he found time to do some writing also, which was important for his future. He wrote two books on the Synoptic Problem, both of which were well received, and one, *The Case Against Q*, made a considerable impact. This book marked the provisional end to a long campaign against Q. Austin had opened the battle with his 1957 article, *On Dispensing with Q*. Its argument, based on Occam's principle, was valid without, however, being effective; Q had been entrenched for more than a century, and would not be put to flight without high explosives. For more than two decades I championed the Farrer Theory, and sometimes thought of Homer's line, 'For Hector alone defended Troy'. I did this principally with the argument from the Minor Agreements, with a high point at the Duke University debate in 1976. I pursued this line with my 1978 article, 'On Putting Q to the Test', and subsequent debates both oral and in print, mostly with Christopher Tuckett. After the launching of the International Q Project, I developed the second argument, from the close similarity between Q's and Matthew's style. I published the evidence in two articles in the American *Journal of Biblical Literature*, 'Is Q a Juggernaut?' and 'Self-Contradiction in the IQP', and promoted it by questioning Howard Kee at the SNTS Conference in Prague. But Mark's book marked the end of my long lone fight. Soon after this I suffered the first of a series of strokes, which virtually put an end to my own scholarly work, and I was happy to have handed the torch on to so worthy a successor.

Chapter 17

THE OLD TESTAMENT

While my central interest had thus been in the New Testament, I had
at the same time been developing thoughts about the Old Testament,
especially the Psalms. I mentioned above that as a student I preferred
Philosophy to Hebrew; and in time I felt increasingly my lack of Hebrew
as a background to the NT. So when I came to Birmingham, I spoke to
John Eaton, the Old Testament teacher in the Theology Department,
and he kindly invited me to sit in on his undergraduate Hebrew class.
John was the gentlest of men, and the students venerated him, fearing
his lightest reproach. He was taking us through the Psalms, on which he
had himself written a short commentary; and I soon felt the fascination
of the study. The standard interpretation was by a German scholar,
Hermann Gunkel: he had divided the Psalms into categories—communal
laments, hymns, individual thanksgivings, and so on. If a psalm used the
pronoun 'we', it was a communal psalm, used in public liturgy; if it used
the pronoun 'I' it was a private prayer, composed by a pious Israelite as
an expression of his personal religion. Gunkel thought this last category
the most spiritually valuable. John, however, gave reasons for thinking
that the I-psalms were for public use also, the speaker being the national
leader, usually the king. This meant that nearly all the psalms were for
liturgical use; and John agreed with a Norwegian scholar, Sigmund
Mowinckel, in thinking that they were mostly used at the great autumn
festival of Tabernacles. I found all this most attractive: I had been trying
to argue that the Gospels were used liturgically, and was looking for
parallels which would help this argument forward. So I soon began to
take up the study on my own, and noticed some interesting features in
Book IV of the Psalter, which comprises Psalms 90–106. Psalms 93,
97 and 99 all begin (in the traditional version) 'The LORD is king', and
there is a similar expression in Psalm 95. Likewise Psalms 98 and 100
share closely similar language with each other, with 96 not far off; each
of the odd-numbered psalms gives rise, in the even-numbered psalms,
to a call to respond to Yahweh's kingship: nature, i.e. the sea and the

world in general, is to rejoice at Yahweh's power of renewal; the nations are to rejoice at his coming in judgement, though this may not be to their comfort. This pattern of alternation was sufficiently regular as to require an explanation; and it struck me that they might have been used for alternating morning and evening use. This seemed to be confirmed by the fact of there being seventeen psalms in the collection; Tabernacles was an eight-day festival, and would need seventeen psalms to cover the evenings and mornings from beginning to end. The Jewish custom was for the festival to begin in the evening, and Psalm 90 was an evening psalm. I put these ideas together in an article as long ago as 1975, and as I had had an encouraging response to my early NT work from Professor Sparks of the *JTS*, I sent it to him; and to my great pleasure he accepted it for publication.

My experience with the SNTS suggested to me that I should learn much, and enjoy doing so, if I could join a similar Old Testament society. Happily there was such an association, the Society for Old Testament Study, the SOTS, known inevitably as 'Sots'. I could belong if I could read the Hebrew Bible, so I was eligible, and began to attend the meetings, with much pleasure. SOTS was a much smaller society than the SNTS, and much less pretentious; it was a British-Irish society, so the meetings were normally conducted only in English. We did have close relations with a similar Dutch society, and from time to time joint meetings were held; but the Dutch were very courteous and spoke English on such occasions.

The Society was much friendlier than SNTS, and it seemed more open to new ideas; and I was surprised that, after belonging for only two years, I was invited to read a paper at the meeting in Hull. John Eaton had been an excellent teacher of Hebrew, and after we had left his undergraduate class, we were given copies of an informal reader which he had put together. This comprised a small selection of articles on interesting passages in the Hebrew Bible; one of these was by an American scholar, Cheryl Exum, about the Song of Songs, also known as the Song of Solomon. I did not find Dr Exum's discussion persuasive, but it introduced me to one of the most fascinating and enigmatic books in Scripture. The Song is apparently a series of alternating love poems by a man and a woman, and the interpretation is obscure. Many Jewish interpreters understand it to be addressed to Queen Sabbath; Roman Catholic scholars commonly see it as spoken to the Virgin Mary; the Authorized Version prints headings at the top of the page, saying that it is about 'the love of Christ for his Church'. Religious people naturally incline to such metaphorical understandings of the text; but these seem to be belied by the language, which often seems suggestively sexual. I was teaching the Song to a class once, and a headmaster present commented, 'If it really is about the love of Christ for his Church, he certainly seems very interested in her breasts'. I was convinced that the interpretation turned on whether the language consisted of precise metaphors (to be understood literally), or was just vaguely 'poetic'. I decided therefore to take this as the subject of my Hull paper, and took some trouble to read a few commentaries, and get the feel of standard opinions. An example of the issue occurs quite early in the text: the bridegroom says, 'Your eyes are doves, bathed in milk, nesting beside a pool, by streams of water'. The Swedish commentator, Gillis Gerleman, remarks that eyes do not resemble doves and that therefore the simile should not be taken literally; indeed he adds that this opinion should not be doubted. I did however doubt it, because the phrase 'bathed in milk' suggested a reference to the whites of the eye, and the 'pool of water' could very suitably be the pupil. The doves, it occurred to me, might well be the eyelids; people say sometimes, 'A girl has but to flutter her eyes', and doves do flutter; also doves are commonly found in pairs, like eyes. So the whole metaphor seemed to be precisely intended, with the milk as the whites of the eye, and the streams as the tear-ducts. This was an original suggestion, and I thought pretty plausible.

I could not get away, however, with a single bright idea, and there were many more difficult passages if I was to be able to persuade a sceptical audience. A little later the bride describes her beloved in a series of comparisons from head to foot, beginning with his hair 'black as a raven', down through his arms to his legs, which are like 'pillars of marble'. Between arms and legs it is said, 'his *me'im* are an *'eshet* of ivory, encrusted with sapphires', or lapis lazuli. There are several difficulties here: me'im is quite a common word, normally meaning the guts or bowels; but here it must refer to something which one can see, so guts is not a possible understanding; it is normal therefore to translate, hopefully, 'his belly'. The word *'eshet* does not occur anywhere else in the Bible, so the translator has to guess; it has been common to give such a rendering as, 'his belly is a plaque of ivory', something nice and flat. Lys, a French critic, comments, even more hopefully, 'This is confirmed by the incrustations, which make one think of blue veins on the surface of the skin'. However, as I said in my paper, close personal inspection revealed no veins visible in this area, and I believe this to be a general anatomical truth. I had noticed that one scholar alleges that the word *'eshet* is close to an Akkadian word meaning a column, and this seemed a better option than 'plaque'. So, I concluded in my paper, 'I asked myself therefore, 'Is there a part of the male body between the arms and the legs which is heavily veined, and which in any way resembles a column of ivory?' The answer comes, 'Yes, indeed, there is; and furthermore, what is a column of ivory but a tusk? And to an enthusiastic bride such as is portrayed in the Song, a tusk might be a very potent symbol'. The *me'im* should therefore be understood thus, and translated euphemistically as "loins", as in a number of cases in Genesis'.

The two most learned members of the Society were John Emerton, Professor of Hebrew at Cambridge, and Wilfred Lambert, Professor of Assyriolgy at Birmingham. Wilfred knew more about Akkadian than anyone else present, and he said he did not know of the word 'eshet ever meaning a column in Akkadian; I had therefore to plug the gap as best I could on the spot, and fortunately remembered a comment by one of the later rabbis, who said that the scroll of the Law was an *'eshet* of ivory. As the scroll was cylindrical in shape, the translation 'column' was quite plausible. John Emerton said generously that he thought the paper was the most entertaining that he had heard at the Society. 'But', he continued, less generously, 'the eyelid is not part of the eye'. I thought this comment was hair-splitting; an ophthalmologist might make such a distinction, but it was not clear that an ancient Hebrew would look at things like that. As often when I had given a paper, I lay awake that night turning over what possible response I might have made, and there, about three in the morning, the ideal text occurred to me. The next morning I happened to find myself standing next to Emerton in the men's room, and thought I would seize the opportunity: 'I thought of a text to answer your point yesterday evening. What about Jezebel, who painted her eyes when she saw Jehu approaching? Surely she painted the eyelids, not the eyeballs?' But Emerton was too good for me: 'The Hebrew says, "She set her eyes in antimony"'.

My argument that the imagery in the Song was precise issued in a satisfactory explanation for the text as a whole; and this I published later in a short book, *The Song of Fourteen Songs*, a commentary on the Hebrew text, with a verse translation of my own. The Song is a love-poem with strongly sexual imagery, and consists of a series of related scenes which describe the romance between the King and his foreign bride. The latter is a dark-skinned Arabian girl (AV: 'I am black but comely'). She arrives with her bridesmaids and is courted by the King; she is taken in an elaborate procession round the city walls, to the admiration of the watchers; she comes to the courtyard where the King is enthroned, and is there married to him; the consummation of the marriage is described; step by step it becomes clear that she is his favourite wife, his 'one-and-only', despite his occasional visits to his harem; she dances before him in a diaphanous dress; and finally she is seen in public as his preferred Queen.

This construction of the poem as a series of scenes leading up to a climax enables us to find a setting for it in Israelite life. In 539 BCE the Persian king Cyrus captured Babylon; and many Jews took the opportunity to return to Palestine. Most of them were men, and it became a problem for them to find suitable wives. In consequence a number of them married foreign girls, and this created serious tensions. Conservatives were scandalized that sometimes their children did not speak Hebrew, and it was feared that the foreign women would lead their husbands astray; there was a demand that all such men should divorce their wives. On the other side there was a liberal party, which felt that foreign brides often became good Israelite wives, and that no such divorces should be enforced. In this situation the liberals produced two propaganda tracts, the Book of Ruth and the Song. Ruth tells the story of a Jew called Elimelech who went into exile in Moab during a famine, and married a Moabite girl, Ruth. When her husband died, Ruth volunteered to accompany her mother-in-law to Palestine, protesting that she would be a faithful Israelite. She showed her loyalty by finding a second husband from the same family, Boaz, not without some sexual cunning. She bore him a son, 'raising up seed to her dead husband' as the saying was. In the course of time Ruth became the ancestress of none other than King David. So the book demonstrates that a Moabite wife can be a faithful Israelite, and have her marriage evidently blessed by Jahweh. In the same way the Song describes how Solomon, the most successful of all the Kings of Israel, took an Arabian princess as his favoured wife and Queen; she shows herself throughout the poem to be deeply attached to him, and at the moment of their sexual union he addresses her, to our surprise, 'My sister, my bride'; their union is understood as having made her a full fellow-Israelite. Thus the liberal party produced two magnificent tracts to make their case, and succeeded in doing so; both Ruth and the Song achieved the dignity of being read out during public worship at Israelite festivals, and so secured their place in the Bible, which is the collection of all such liturgical texts.

Chapter 18

THE PSALMS

John Eaton introduced me to the study of the Psalter, and Book IV was only the first collection on which I produced a new theory. There are five books in the Psalter, and their division is not random: Books I, IV, and V all prefer to refer to God by his name Jahweh, while Books II and III prefer the Hebrew word for God, *Elohim*. Most of these psalms have brief headings at their beginning: almost all the Psalms in Book I are headed 'For David'; Psalms 42–49 in Book II, and Psalms 84–85 and 87–88 in Book III are headed 'For the Sons of Korah'; Psalms 50 and 80–83 in Book III are headed 'For Asaph'; in Book V Psalms 120–34 are headed 'Songs of Ascents'; there is a second David collection in Book II, Psalms 51–72.

The first collection to attract my attention was the Korah Psalms. The sons of Korah were a guild of priests in Jerusalem in later centuries, inferior to the family of the High Priest. It is generally supposed that their psalms, like the others, were composed for use in Jerusalem; but Psalm 42 contains the surprising verse, 'I will remember thee from the land of Jordan, the Hermons, the little hill'; and this seems to indicate somewhere different from Jerusalem. That city is not close to the Jordan river; and the Hermons are a group of mountains on the frontier with Lebanon, two hundred miles to the north. There is an ancient shrine in this district, called Dan, once the site of worship much disapproved of in Jerusalem. Dan lies on a spur, 'a small hill' jutting out from Mount Hermon, and it is close to this spur that one of the sources of the Jordan rises. Mount Hermon is an enormous mountain, ten thousand feet in height, four times as high as Mount Zion. With its height and its river it had been a sacred site for many centuries before the Israelites came to the land. It was natural for them to take over the holy site from their predecessors, and Dan was a centre of Israelite worship before Solomon built the Temple at Jerusalem. Psalm 42 also says, 'Deep calleth to deep at the sound of the waterfalls'; there are hardly any waterfalls in Palestine, and those that there are lie in the north of the country close to Dan. Furthermore Psalm 48 speaks of the City of God as being 'noble in height, on the frontiers of the north'; such a description would not suit Jerusalem either for height or for location, but it would suit Dan in both respects. Psalm 42 describes the singer as 'I go mourning', and it would be suitable to suppose, with John Eaton, that the speaker was the Israelite King leading the annual pilgrimage to the shrine of Dan.

By 1980 I was beginning thus to form a theory to cover all the Korah Psalms from 42 to 49. Psalm 42 was the psalm sung by the king and his court poet en route to the national festival at Dan. Psalm 43 implied a sacrifice at dawn the following morning. Psalms 44–49 were the liturgy for the succeeding days of the festival. While I was working out the ramifications of this idea, I had a term of study leave, and with it the opportunity to read up the account of the excavation of Dan by the Israeli archaeologist Biran. I found this intensely exciting, for he had uncovered things which I had predicted from words in the Psalms text. He included photographs and line drawings; one of the former was of the pilgrimage road to the City gate, 'cast up' from stones to permit the passage of wagons and chariots. One of the line drawings was of steps up to a sacrificial area made of large stones above the City. Another showed three bases, carved like pumpkins, on which once stood pillars flanking the royal throne. This was in line with Psalm 45 where the King is anointed and enthroned, and married to his new wife. The Psalm speaks of stringed instruments out of ivory palaces making him glad; so it is clear that the throne stood in the 'gate', that is the public courtyard inside the City gate, with a palace behind it, and an orchestra playing through an open window. I was sufficiently fascinated by this that I wrote to Biran, and arranged to visit Israel and to go and see Tell-Dan. Biran received me with courtesy, but he was sceptical of my idea of the palace being behind the throne; he commented, 'But I have already uncovered the palace on the other side of the City entrance. In any case a palace would never be built directly behind the City gate'. I replied that his palace might well be the building provided for the womenfolk, which is also referred to in the text; and that there was a royal palace behind the gateway at Jezreel. 'Jezreel has not been excavated', he said; but I pointed out that in the text of 2 Kings Jehu 'stood in the gateway' and called to the eunuchs to throw Jezebel down; which they did, and the horses trampled her. So it is clear that at Jezreel the palace was next to the gateway. Biran replied somewhat reluctantly, 'You certainly know your texts'. He was helpful to me in suggesting things I might look for in the site at Tell-Dan.

Soon afterwards I took a bus up to Upper Galilee, where I was able to stay at a kibbutz hotel not far from the site. There was only one other guest in the hotel, a British businessman, who shared my table at dinner. I asked what he was selling, and he produced from his pocket a handkerchief which apparently contained about a hundred diamonds; these were in fact small plastic capsules, filled with some fluid which emitted beta-rays. These shone faintly in the dark, and he hoped to sell them to be incorporated into Israeli army rifles as foresights and backsights, which would enable the rifles to be aimed in the dark at an enemy without being seen. The next morning I set out on the road to where I could see the three peaks of the towering Mount Hermon against the sky. I came round the bend, and there was the 'little hill', with the City's ruins on it. I crossed a rivulet, one of the streams which was to combine with others into the River Jordan, and came to the City gate. As with all Israelite towns, the circle of the City wall slightly overlapped, enabling the gate to be set at right angles, so that the defenders could drop rocks or boiling oil on any enemy with a battering ram. I walked through the gate, and there was Biran's courtyard, just as described in his article. There stood the three surviving bases, out of the original four on which were stood the pillars vaulting the royal throne. The text of Psalm 45 has a note at its head, 'At the Lilies'. I had originally misunderstood this to imply that the throne stood in a garden, but I now realized that the 'Lilies' were ornate capitals at the head of pillars which once surrounded the site; such ornate capitals had been invented in Egypt, and had been taken over for royal use by Israelite kings. The Bible describes Solomon as building his palace with pillars, 'and above was lily-work'; the design was in time taken over by the Greeks, who used it for the capitals of Ionic pillars, likening them to rams' horns rather than the curling lily petals envisaged by the Israelites.

The text of Psalm 45 speaks of the bride as the 'daughter of Tyre', and this almost certainly means Jezebel, daughter of Ittobaal, king of Tyre, who married Ahab King of (northern) Israel around 850 BCE. This enables us to imagine the scene in some detail. There is Ahab sitting on his throne. Some distance in front of him is a worn stone which will have been where the Queen made her obeisance to him on their marriage. On the King's left is a stone bench, which Biran uncovered, and on this will have been seated Obadiah, Ahab's General, and perhaps other nobles. The text mentions a number of wealthy Israelites who have come with their gifts, to 'smooth her face', i.e. to win her favour. I walked through the roadway into the town, and there on the right was the royal palace as I had sited it. On the left was the Queen's palace, where the text describes the new Queen as withdrawing to change into her cloth of gold dress. In this she was to be carried over by eunuchs in a palanquin for her wedding night. It was easy to imagine the cheering crowds as she was brought 'with joy and gladness' for the occasion. Among these, but not perhaps so cheerful, would be Elijah from Tishbeh, Naboth of Jezreel, and Jehu son of Nimshi. But to most people a wedding to a Tyrian princess implied a diplomatic triumph; Ahab now had a powerful ally, and was himself to be reckoned as an influential monarch. I went on up the roadway to the top of the town, and there were Biran's steps leading up to the paving stones of the sacrificial area referred to in Psalm 43. I returned to the gateway and found a stone pathway leading round the outside of the City wall; soon I reached the source of the river, which was celebrated in Psalm 46 as 'making glad the City of God'. This psalm also refers to the burning of enemy chariots and weapons, and behind the spring was a mound which I suspected contained the remains of much charred wood. The pathway continued round the City, and would have provided a suitable road for the great procession described in Psalm 48, which celebrates the City of God with a circumambulation by the people. As I went along this path, I was impressed by the volumes of water which streamed down the hillside where the town had been. This was suggestive in another way: Psalm 88 is the prayer of a representative of the people who has volunteered to pass the night alone in an underground chamber, partly flooded. I would not be able to find the precise location of such a chamber, but clearly the streaming water was evidence that such floods did indeed occur. In this way I had an explanation for the Korah Psalms series: there was an archaeological site for almost all the places referred to in the text; and the psalms ran in a believable series from 42, the pilgrimage psalm, to 49, a psalm anticipating victory over Israel's enemies. A similar progression could be identified in Psalms 84 to 89, the former being a second pilgrimage psalm and the latter an anticipation of triumph.

In time I was to publish four volumes commenting on different collections of psalms, and the first of these was *The Psalms of the Sons of Korah*. Some years later I had a letter from Robert Gordon, Professor at Cambridge. He told me he had used the Korah psalms as the text for one of his seminars each year, and had always got the students to read my book. He added the dubious compliment, 'I admired the magnifiqueness of your theory'. At first I took this at its face value; but reflection made me suspect a more subtle and less flattering intention. Like the Charge of the Light Brigade at Balaclava, my theory was magnificent but not the genuine article—'C'est magnifique, mais ce n'est pas la guerre'. The response was characteristic of a professional: he would not have made his students read the book if he did not think it was good, but he could not bring himself to say that it was persuasive, let alone simply magnificent.

The verdict on my work by the top people has always been double-edged. An American scholar, David Aune, said to me once, 'I have never read a good review of your work. I do not mean that the reviewers pan it, but they do not engage with your arguments'. This was exactly what I had often felt myself. David made a further comment: 'Your theories always seem to fit the facts too well. It's like a man with a one-armed bandit; if he pulls three apples or three oranges, he has won: but if he pulls eight apples, you know that someone has been monkeying with the machine'. It seemed as if I was caught in a Catch-22 situation.

My work on the Psalms had a good effect on my reputation in more than one way. It helped me of course to have had a considerable and original book published; but it also meant that when I listened to other people's papers at SOTS meetings, I was in a position to ask informed and searching questions. My Psalms theories had taken me into areas of the OT quite distant from the Psalms, and as I had done the thinking for myself and read quite widely, I was often able to show flaws in the speaker's argument; it was a surprising compliment to be told that I was one of the most feared members of the Society. I was pleased soon afterwards to be invited to give a second paper. I took as my subject the Psalms of Asaph, Psalms 50 and 73–83. These psalms are singular in referring a number of times to God's people as 'Joseph'. Psalm 80 indeed mentions in particular the tribes of Ephraim, Benjamin, and Manasseh. These tribes lay together in central Israel, to the north of Judah, which was an independent kingdom with its capital at Jerusalem. For some centuries the Joseph tribes had their own religious centre at Bethel and a king of their own, with his capital at Samaria. If these psalms had been written at Jerusalem, it would be extraordinary for there to have been no mention of Judah. The interesting thing is that in several of the Asaph Psalms an account is given of details in Israel's history which differ markedly from the account we have in the Pentateuch. It is unlikely that the psalmist deliberately or accidentally made changes from the official version; rather we should think that the Psalms version represents an earlier, independent account composed in Bethel, and later transferred to Jerusalem. When the Assyrians attacked northern Israel in the 730s they destroyed the shrine of Bethel, and the priests fled to Jerusalem, taking their laws, their historical traditions and their psalms with them.

The case for the place of origin and early date of these psalms seemed strong and well-evidenced, and I was able to close my paper with a challenging sentence, 'You've got to hand it to Wellhausen'. Julius Wellhausen had been the principal author of the standard theory of the Pentateuch in the 1870s. He saw four sources as underlying the text: J, the work of the Jahwist, E, the work of the Elohist, D, the Deuteronomist, and P, the Priestly author. Wellhausen thought that the E-traditions came from northern Israel, and spoke of God as Elohim. This theory had commanded wide acceptance, but since 1930 doubts had been raised about the E-source, though the other sources were still generally accepted. I was able therefore with my evidence from the Asaph Psalms to show that Wellhausen was right after all: here was a body of text using the name Elohim for God, coming from northern Israel, and comprising a version of the historical traditions earlier than those we have in the Pentateuch. I knew at once that the paper had gone down well. It was just the kind of thing to please the Society, an original and provocative hypothesis calling in question a widespread judgement. This time there were no difficult questions from Professors Emerton and Lambert. After a minute's silence my friend Lester Grabbe made an innocuous suggestion, and I was able to cash in on my advantage: 'Thank you for an interesting suggestion; but as you know, Lester, I like to stick to facts. I should not wish to descend to hypotheses and speculations. That be far from me'. As I was notorious for bold hypotheses, this was obviously absurd and raised a good laugh.

Soon after this, I published *The Psalms of Asaph and the Pentateuch*; my friends David Clines and Philip Davies, the editors of the Sheffield Academic Press, were welcoming to my proposal, as they had been also to *The Psalms of the Sons of Korah*, and earlier to my two-volume commentary on St Luke's Gospel. The Asaph book was interesting, as it not only explained these particular psalms, but also offered with their aid an insight into early Israelite history. But there were further psalms which might be of similar interest, those headed 'For David'; these were in two series, Pss. 3–41, and 51–72. This second series was especially inviting. Scholars who had studied the David stories in the Books of Samuel had described the later parts of the tradition as 'the Succession Narrative'. This began with David's adultery with Bathsheba, and his subsequent murder of her husband Uriah. Bathsheba became mother of Solomon, but the Prophet Nathan foretold that God would punish David for what he had done: the sword would never depart from his house; and in the story following one after another of his sons is killed, culminating in the rebellion and death of his favourite Absalom. Now it so happens that Psalm 51 is headed with a short historical note linking it with David's affair with Bathsheba, and Psalm 72, the last of the series, is headed 'For Solomon'. It looked to me as if this could hardly be accidental: the stories about David were probably recited at Israelite festivals to seal the people's loyalty to David and his son Solomon, and it would be very suitable for a court poet to compose psalms which would be responses to the narratives. The wording of Psalm 51 seemed to confirm this, for God is prayed to deliver David from blood-guilt, such as would fall on him after the death of Uriah; Psalm 72 similarly is a prayer for the 'king's son', that he may reign with peace and justice, such as obtained in Solomon's reign. One major test was available for the theory: the crisis of David's reign was Absalom's rebellion, and its defeat in 'the forest of Ephraim'. Now there is one psalm in the series, no. 68, which celebrates a victory in battle at a place called Zalmon; and we know of this place as standing in wooded country in the area of the tribe of Ephraim. Also this psalm contains several references to details of the situation given in the Second Book of Samuel. In the Psalter this second David collection was followed by a note, 'The Prayers of David, the son of Jesse, are ended'; so I called my book *The Prayers of David*. It would have been neat and convenient if I could have worked out a similar theory for the first David collection; but the evidence was not so clear, and I knew better than to force it. Later I returned to this problem, and published in *JSOT* an account of Psalms 23 and 24 as comments on David's capture of Jerusalem. Meanwhile I turned my attention to the psalms in Book V; and I was delighted to find a close parallel between the so-called 'Songs of Ascents' and the Book of Nehemiah. It looked as though the Book of Nehemiah consisted of a sequence of narratives covering Nehemiah's return ('Ascent') from Babylon to Jerusalem; and that Pss. 120–34 had been written as a series of liturgical responses to these events narrated during worship in the Temple. This enabled me to produce my fourth Psalms commentary, *The Psalms of the Return*.

My studies of the Psalter had thus indicated that the Psalms presented a series of independent and mostly earlier insights into the history of the Israelite people. Their departure from Egypt and their journeys through the wilderness are described in the books of Exodus and Numbers; but an earlier account of the same story is available in the Psalms of Asaph (73–83). The Book of Judges gives an extremely hostile account of the shrine at Dan; but the Psalms of the Sons of Korah show what worship at Dan had really been like in the time of Ahab. The events of David's reign are set out in 2 Samuel 12 to 1 Kings 1; but a contemporary response to the same material is given in the second David psalm sequence, 51–72. The history of the Israelite monarchies is given in 2 Kings; but we have earlier insights into this from the psalms, especially the Korah and Asaph sequences. The Hebrew Bible closes the national narrative with the story of the Return under Nehemiah; and here finally we have a contemporary response to the narrative, in the Songs of Ascents (120–34).

My succession of papers addressed to the SOTS, coupled with the publication of the Psalms commentaries, led to an unexpected honour.

The list of Presidents of the SOTS comprises the names of all the most famous British scholars of the subject since the beginning of the century; and in my time the Presidents had been a succession of learned men (and one woman), most of them also gifted with a ready wit which made meetings a pleasure to attend. It had never occurred to me that I myself might one day be numbered among such a company, and I was amazed, therefore, when, as we walked together down the corridor after a paper, Katharine Dell, the Secretary of the Society, told me that I had been elected President for 2001. There were a number of people who might well have been thought of before me, and I felt duly humble. Needless to say, I accepted with alacrity: here was recognition such as I had not known before. My presidency would cover two meetings, one at Leeds in January, and the other at my own University in July. I had also to chair a meeting to select speakers for the programme, and to deliver a Presidential Address, which should be an occasion of some dignity and interest. But before all this a traumatic event occurred which nearly prevented my taking up the post at all. In October Clare and I had been having a short holiday in the Quantocks, when on our last day I suffered a fall, which put me in hospital between life and death for some days, and ended with my having lost the sight of my left eye, and being too weak for some time even to walk. It was touch and go whether I should be able to get to Leeds in January, or manage once I got there. So it was with huge relief and much thankfulness that, in the end, with Clare there to help me, all went well.

For my Presidential Address I had chosen to speak on the well-known enigma of Isaiah 53. I had been working on this passage, which has puzzled people for many years. Various solutions have been proposed as to the identity of the Suffering Servant, some proposing historical characters, some symbolic; but I had come to the conclusion that the man referred to was Jehoiachin, who was King of Judah when the City of Jerusalem was taken by the Babylonians. It seemed to me that every detail of this famous chapter corresponded with things which we knew about this king, from his youth in the Temple at Jerusalem to his condemnation to life imprisonment in Babylon. I wanted to begin with a light opening, so I mentioned Robert Gordon's 'magnifiqueness' comment, and said that I would be making a bold—some might say rash—attack on a well-defended position. I drew the paper to a conclusion on the same theme: 'So there go my six hundred brave lancers, in their buff coats, with their sabres drawn; it is time to hear the Russian guns volley and thunder'. On this occasion the guns were less damaging than at Balaclava, and the Society went happily to the bar for a drink. The paper was published a few months later in *Vetus Testamentum*, the premier OT journal.

I presided over the papers at the two meetings with sufficient humour to keep the Society happy, and there was only one moment in which I was faced with a difficulty. Gordon Wenham, a friendly and humble evangelical, spoke in the course of his paper of Christianity as a religion superior to Judaism. This remark was against the custom of the Society, because we had Jewish members, and such comparisons were out of place in discussions of scholarship. So I thought I ought to comment during the question time, and mentioned a lecture given in Birmingham by Robert Carroll, a previous President of the Society. He had listed a number of occasions in which the Bible had been used for cruel and immoral purposes; someone had commented afterwards that most of his instances had been taken from the Old Testament; Carroll replied, 'The New Testament *is* shorter, but it is worse: it contains two things not found in the Old Testament, anti-Semitism and hell'. Wilfred Lambert took me to task afterwards for objecting to Wenham's comparison. He said. 'Christianity *is* a religion superior to Judaism'. I do in fact agree with Lambert, and think that people ought to be able to say things which others find objectionable; but in this context I felt it was close to discourtesy, and needed my intervention.

My interest in Isaiah 53, however, soon fanned out into a more general theory of the structure of the book. I noticed that the book divided into eight sections, each opening with a new vision or other introduction. These eight sections covered the same topics as the Korah psalms, and in the same order. It seemed natural to conclude that Isaiah had been used to provide prophecies through an eight-day liturgy at the autumn festival, just like the psalms. Just as the Korahite Levites were given a slot each day in the autumn festival to sing their traditional psalms, so the Isaiah prophetic community was given a similar opportunity to recite the traditional prophecies suited to the day's theme. I wrote this idea up as a book, *Isaiah as Liturgy*, and this was published in 2004, the first of a series of SOTS monographs. Not everyone was persuaded by it; but I was rewarded, at long last, by one really positive review, by John Sawyer, a respected scholar, who described it as 'fascinating', 'original', and 'persuasive'.

Chapter 19

VISITING LECTURESHIPS

As a result of my regular attendance at the annual SNTS Conferences, I made friends with a good number of scholars, often because their thinking was similar to mine. Many universities have funds for occasional visiting lecturers, and over the years I was invited to give such lectures, both in Britain and abroad, especially in Scandinavia. One such friend was Ruth Edwards, who taught in Aberdeen, and she recommended me as an interesting speaker to William Johnstone, her OT Professor. I accepted the invitation, and was surprised to be given an air-ticket and met by Johnstone at Aberdeen Airport. It was a busy day, he told me: I was to lecture at 11.00; there was an eminent scholar in an allied subject speaking in the afternoon; and in the evening a presentation to Howard Marshall, the NT Professor, who had attracted the largest number of post-graduates to the University from America. I gave as my lecture an earlier form of the Two Missions thesis, which I have described above as the topic of my Inaugural. I was sufficiently experienced to know what sort of response this might draw: there would be Staff members present and students, who had been drafted in to hear the visitor; Staff members would think it important to show their students that they knew as much as the speaker, so they would make a courteous remark and then try to ask an effective question. To my surprise, the first question was asked by a mature lady in the front row, who said, 'I have never heard so persuasive an account of New Testament origins. Can you think of any weakness in the argument?' I could have answered that I had recently submitted the lecture as an article for *JTS*, and it had been rejected; but I did not feel that honesty compelled me to be as candid as that. Otherwise the question-time passed off easily.

After lunch it was the turn of the eminent scholar, who turned out to be the lady who had asked the first question. The lecture was difficult in every way. The afternoon was steaming hot, but if we opened the windows there was the constant clatter of the lunch plates being washed up, which made it difficult to hear her. She was not an Old Testament scholar, but had elected to speak about the Book of Numbers. This book, she alleged, could be divided into eighteen sections, of which number one corresponded to number eighteen, two to seventeen, and so on. I found this suggestion unconvincing, and was confident that most other people would feel the same about it; in consequence, when she finished there would be a long silence for lack of questions. My expectation was exactly fulfilled. Johnstone thanked her courteously, and asked something innocuous, and silence followed. As she had been so generous in response to my lecture in the morning, I felt I should plug the gap if I could, and asked a rather meaningless question. This was received with more warmth than I had expected, and when she saw me afterwards she thanked me enthusiastically and said that she thought we should correspond. This was not at all what I wanted, and I subsequently received a series of letters pressing similar arguments which I found quite unpersuasive. Howard Marshall invited me to give a paper to his post-graduate seminar the next day; there were about fifteen men present, and not a Scot among them. These were the Americans for whose fees the Vice-Chancellor was so grateful. Howard mentioned that I had resigned my Orders, and after the talk one of those present asked me why I studied the New Testament. He seemed quite surprised when I said it was the search for the truth; so often the only reason has seemed to be to support Christian belief.

At SNTS Meetings those invited to give a paper choose their own topic; but the University of Leuven used to organise a series of Journées bibliques each year, at which a single theme was decided in advance. In 1980 the theme chosen was 'John and the Synoptics'. For many years it had been a disputed question whether John knew, and radically changed, the Synoptics, or whether he had quite independent sources. Neirynck, who was the guiding force behind the enterprise, was himself convinced that John did so know his predecessors' work, and set out to persuade the conference of the rightness of his view. He began with a paper in which he listed all the universities whose New Testament teachers agreed with him; and I was flattered that he included among these the University of Birmingham: as neither Neville Birdsall nor David Parker had published a view on this question, the view of the University of Birmingham must have been my view. A number of well-known scholars were asked to give plenary papers, but an important element of the conference was the division into three Seminars, respectively speaking English, French, and German. I was asked to be Chairman of the English Seminar, which involved my giving its opening paper, and I did this by commenting on the whole opening section of John's Gospel down to the middle of chapter 2. With my Two Missions theory I was in a position to explain why John, who was a Pauline, should depreciate Peter and the family of Jesus, the leaders of the Jerusalem church. The paper went down well, and I felt that the same arguments could be applied to the next chapter and a half; so I submitted both my Seminar paper and a further article for publication in the Proceedings. Thus I had a commentary in print on Jn 1–4, and was ready to extend this to the entire Gospel. Sadly, however, the three strokes I sustained between 2003 and 2005 prevented my completing this project.

As I came out of the Seminar room in Leuven, I was greeted by two scholars, both of them from Sweden, though neither actually Swedish. One of these, Chrys Caragounis, was a Greek, teaching New Testament at Lund; he expressed admiration for my pronunciation of Greek, and asked me where I had learned to speak Greek properly. There are two normal pronunciations of the Greek language by NT critics: English scholars pronounce the letter eta as 'ee', as in 'feet', whereas German scholars tend to pronounce it as in 'fate'. Some people have adopted a third option, as in 'fair'. Chrys had studied the pronunciations presupposed in manuscripts going back to very early times, and he was persuaded that New Testament Greek was pronounced very close to modern Greek. I had become used to this because it was used by Neville Birdsall, and when I queried it to him he referred me to a member of the Classics Department at Birmingham, who confirmed his opinion. So I had fallen into the way of following 'modern' Greek usage, which treats the eta in the English manner, but other sounds quite differently.

The other person waiting for me was an old friend, René Kieffer. René had been born in Luxembourg, and had had difficulty in evading conscription into the occupying German army during the War. A good Catholic, René had joined the Dominican Order, the Blackfriars; and in time he was sent to Sweden to convert the Lutherans to Catholicism, teaching New Testament in Swedish universities. To assist him the Church sent also a woman missionary to evangelise Swedish women; and the two cooperated so well that in course of time they fell in love, and decided to laicise and marry. René had now been promoted to be Professor at Uppsala, the most ancient university in Sweden. As such, in 1990 he was required to find a speaker for the next year's meeting of the Swedish Exegetical Society, and thought he would like to invite me. I was delighted to accept, but I was somewhat taken aback by the letter I had from him three weeks later. It so happened that the next year was the 450th anniversary of the translation of the Bible into Swedish, and the committee would like me to give my lecture to a comparison of the recent (1981) version of the NT with that of 1917.

This was a formidable undertaking, for I had not a word of Swedish, and even if I were able to enrol on a crash course, I could still scarcely hope to read and compare these two versions within a few months. However, I was not one to duck a difficult challenge, and I soon decided on a strategy which would enable me to carry out the commission. I thought of twelve short passages where the translation was in doubt, but where I was clear what I thought myself. I sent to René to ask for photocopies of the two translations of these twelve passages; when they arrived, I had recourse to the Swedish dictionary in the Library, and was quickly able to puzzle out which way the two translations had jumped. By the time my visit to Uppsala was only a month away I had my lecture prepared, and the twelve passages set out in Greek and in the two Swedish versions on sheets ready for circulation. Even so I should not have been able to get away with pretending that I could understand Swedish, since I could not pronounce a word of it. In this situation I had a stroke of luck. Fortune does sometimes favour the brave, and I had a visit at this time from a Swedish friend, Tord Fornberg. Tord was not a high-flying NT scholar, but I had met him several times at SNTS meetings, and he had come to Birmingham to consult with scholars in the Christian-Islamic Institute at Selly Oak. He kindly read through my passages with me and tutored me in pronouncing the words in an authentic way. With this training, and my ability to mimic the depressed actors in Ingmar Bergman films, I could give a passable imitation of a genuine knowledge of the language.

After so much preparation, the great day went off quite successfully. I was given the first slot in the morning, and questions were postponed to the late afternoon; but Professor Riesenfeld, the veteran Jewish Swedish scholar, who had been responsible for the 1981 translation, was sitting in the front row and I knew from René that he did not respond kindly to criticism, so the occasion had its *frisson*. But in fact at the end he made some appreciative comments to me privately. The second paper was then given by a German OT scholar, and here I was in luck. He took as his subject an area which I had myself studied in some depth; so when the question time came I was able to engage with him, with confidence and fluency, showing knowledge of the Hebrew text of Psalm 132 and some allied passages. This did my reputation no harm, as I was seen to be competent in the Old Testament as well as the New. In the afternoon there was a third lecture, by Professor Albrektson, a Swedish OT scholar. After this the questions were directed to me in turn; and now life was not so easy. An oldish man, probably a Lutheran pastor, who had kept up his scholarly interests, asked me a long question which involved him in reading out a considerable passage in Hebrew. This left me in disarray as although I can normally read Hebrew and understand it, it is not the same when it is read to you in a strange accent. I picked out the word *mal'akh*, which means a messenger, and which recurred a number of times; but I still had no idea what the passage was or what its relevance was to any forthcoming question. Luckily the man was sitting quite close to me, and casting my eye over his Bible, I could pick out the words 'Num. 21' at the head of the page. I remembered that Numbers 21 tells the story of Balaam's ass, and of course about the angel of the Lord who obstructed him. So it was this divine messenger who kept being referred to, and when we finally reached the question, I was able to show a fluent knowledge of the passage. Phew!

This was not, however, the end of my trials. As we left the hall, René said to me, 'Now we go over for this evening's banquet. I thought it would be nice if you would make the speech'. I had no objection to making a speech, but I would have much preferred to be given an hour or two to prepare it. As it was, I was given a seat on the high table between two Professors' wives, Mrs Hartmann and Mrs Riesenfeld. These two ladies had been well brought up, especially Mrs Riesenfeld, who had attended a finishing school in England. They both knew that their task was to keep the conversation flowing, and not allow any embarrassing silences. So I was searching earnestly for what on earth I could say in my speech against a barrage of continuing small talk. We finally reached a point where Mrs Riesenfeld said, 'And how is the new airport at Stansted getting on?' I thought, 'Blow the new airport at Stansted'; and at this point silence was called and I had to begin. The wise advice on such occasions is to tell an anecdote, and I had recourse to an evening some years before which René Kieffer and I had shared after a conference, at a fair in Oxford. René had induced me to go on the dodgems with him, and he drove with such ferocity that I emerged badly shaken. He then took me up a series of ladders in an enormous tent to a platform with a pile of mats on the right side and a copper runway sloping down at sixty degrees on the left. René went down first with the velocity of a bullet, and I followed, prudently slowing my pace with my shoe against the edge. At the bottom René confided to me that he had a confession to make: 'I put my foot out against the side'. I had to admit that I had done the same.

Some weeks later there was a sequel to this story. My cousin Derek's son Peter was marrying a Swedish American bride, Suzanne, and we were bidden to the wedding. In the service the bride's father read the lesson, 1 Corinthians 13, in Swedish, and Clare, who had studied Old English at Oxford, was interested to notice links between the Swedish and Anglo-Saxon. Standing in line waiting to speak to the couple, we found ourselves opposite Suzanne's father, and Clare said, 'I enjoyed your reading of the lesson'. This gave him the impression that we could understand Swedish. Clare then continued, 'We were in Uppsala last month. Michael was lecturing on different Swedish translations of the Bible'. So now he *knew* I could speak Swedish! I felt I should rise to the occasion, but all I could remember was the last of my twelve passages: 'Trembling and astonishment had come over them'. So I said, in a sepulchral voice, 'Baevan och Bestoertning hadde kommit oever mij (me)'. The father bowed low, and said, 'I hope I did not make too many errors in my reading'.

I found my ideas met with a readier response in Scandinavia than elsewhere, and I also made friends more easily there. Earlier I had been invited by Mogens Müller to give some lectures in Copenhagen, and he and his wife Lisbet entertained us most hospitably. We were also kindly treated by his colleague Niels Hyldahl and his wife Sol. We became friends with both families, and were pleased to entertain them in Birmingham in 1994. Then in 1995 I was invited to Finland. I had two special friends in the country: Heikki Räisänen, one of the most distinguished NT scholars in the world, was Professor in Helsinki, and Karl-Gustav Sandelin was Professor in Åbo. I gave two lectures in each University, one on the IQP and the other on the Ebionites (see Chapter 21). While we were in Helsinki we were entertained each evening to dinner with one or other of the staff, and Clare especially appreciated being taken one day to see the home of Sibelius. We then went to Åbo, and at one point, when we were standing on a bridge across the river, Clare happened to ask which way the river was actually flowing, for the wind was blowing the surface of the water upstream; this delighted me, as it provided an ideal image for St Mark's Gospel, where the underlying theology is that of the Jerusalem church, but some of the surface details reveal Mark as a disciple of Paul. After my lectures in Åbo, we were invited to stay with the Sandelins in their country home at Ekenas, which we much enjoyed.

While speaking of my lecturing abroad, I should mention the Swan Hellenic cruises, for which I was invited to be Guest Lecturer six times between 1981 and 1990: five times round the Eastern Mediterranean, and once up the Danube. I was still a clergyman in 1981, and one Sunday in April I had a phone call from Anthony Harvey, who had been a support to me over the DD. Anthony had engaged to be Lecturer and Chaplain on an Easter cruise, and was due to leave on Wednesday. Sadly his wife had fallen ill, and he was looking for someone who could take his place on the cruise. It would involve some twenty talks in all, of varied lengths, for which he would bring me the books, so I could prepare them; also I would be expected to take the church services. I was happy to accept the challenge, and Clare agreed, somewhat hesitantly, to come too. Anthony was as good as his word, and we set off on the Tuesday, to fly to Dubrovnik the next morning. I never saw Dubrovnik: I was down in my cabin, reading feverishly. The next day the ship went round Mount Athos, and I had been given the task of commenting on the forty-eight monasteries and sketes which were to be seen. The whole thing took about three hours, and it was hard to keep the interest up. As we passed a Russian Orthodox monastery, the ship's captain, a kindly Greek with a limited command of English, told me helpfully, 'Before the War, there were four thousand monkeys here'. Even with the aid of a gin and tonic, I was relieved when we moved on. During the next fortnight, I gave lectures on topics which included the great mosques in Istanbul, the mosaics in the Church of Our Saviour in Chora, the Greek War of Independence, the relief carving of a ship on Rhodes, and the catacombs at Syracuse. This last was somewhat of a tour de force: at the beginning of the cruise, one of the other lecturers on board, Professor Kirk, had kindly offered to help me out by giving the first long lecture, which should have been mine. But in Sicily the time now came for him to call in this favour. At breakfast, thinking that he and his wife would prefer to go off for a swim, he asked me to take his lecture for him, and handed me a guidebook. This was in Italian, and the coach was leaving for the catacombs within the hour. I did my best.

Despite my precarious knowledge, I was pleased to find that I was a popular lecturer. The other lecturers were specialists in their subject, and sometimes overloaded their talks with facts; whereas, as an Extramural Lecturer I had found that a sense of humour went a long way. Even more important was that a speaker should feel for his subject. People can absorb only a limited amount of information; what they want is to experience the event with something of its original impact. So, for example, I would quote a verse found by Jan Morris on a cross at Gallipoli:

> God took our Norman, it was his will;
> Forget him? No, we never will,

whose very simplicity gave eloquence to their sense of loss. Or, to show that there was a positive side even to Greek slavery, I would cite this epitaph written by a master for his handmaid, 'Zosime, who before was a slave only in the body, has now in her body also found freedom'. So, besides conveying information, at times I drew from the audience both laughter and tears.

In the eighties, Swan's was still concerned with its original vision, to provide a genuine experience of the Hellenic world centuries earlier. It still hired a Greek ship, Orpheus, one of moderate size, accommodating no more than three hundred passengers. It had not yet commissioned the larger Minerva, which could take many more and became more simply a means of making money. The firm was symbolised by the formidable figure of Doreen Goodrick, the Cruise Director, who insisted on discipline alike from her staff and her passengers. There were normally five Guest Lecturers on each cruise, a doyen classical scholar, an archaeologist, a clergyman, and in the spring a botanist. Some of these were well-known people: Bedel (pron. Beadle) Stanford, an Anglo-Irish Professor of Classics, used to come regularly. Among the clergy were Robert Runcie, later Archbishop of Canterbury, and David Jenkins, Bishop of Durham. The Swan organization was brilliantly efficient, but there were occasional misadventures. On one occasion Professor Stanford took a party of us from Venice by coach to see the Palladian villas on the River Brenta; the trip was unfortunate, as when we reached the village of Stra we found the Villa Pisani was closed. This was in fact the second disappointment of the day, and one of the Swanners was so incensed that he reduced the girl courier to tears. I felt that some distraction was desirable, so I announced to the coach that I had composed a short epic in honour of Professor Stanford, which I would recite in an English translation:

> Dear Bedel, we all cry Hurrah;
> You're the sweetest Professor by far.
> And we don't care a pin
> That we couldn't get in
> To the Villa Pisani in Stra.

With a large and varied public, you were always liable to find someone in the audience who knew more than you did. A month before the cruise lecturers would be sent a list of the talks required, with three columns: A, I would like to give this talk; B, I don't mind; C, I would rather not. Then a fortnight later came the programme, which might bear little relation to one's preferences. I had never seen the Gulf of Kotor in Yugoslavia, and had marked it 'C'; but the programme ran, 'The boat will go round the Gulf of Kotor. Dr Goulder will point out the sights and give a short history of Montenegro'! In Istanbul I was assigned the church of St Sergius and St Bacchus, built by Justinian. When I had said all I knew about the squinches and pendentives of this building, I filled in with some colourful detail about the Empress Theodora. As we left the church, a cultured man said to me, 'So you do not agree with Procopius?' I am ashamed to say that I have never read Procopius, though I agreed with Peter Brown, whose book I had read on the subject. I was also assigned the lecture on the Dardanelles Campaign, and the Cruise Manager kindly warned me, 'We have two Generals on board'. As we left Saloniki, he said to me reassuringly, 'One of the Generals has had a heart attack, and the other has stayed in Athens to look after him'. So when I had completed the sad tale of 1915, I relaxed a little and concluded, 'Could matters have gone any better? Had General Goulder been in command, things would have been far otherwise', adding one or two pieces of wisdom after the event. Seated next to Clare at dinner that night was a man of military bearing, who said in a friendly way, 'My name is John Stanier'. I thought immediately, 'General Sir John Stanier'. He said to me afterwards, 'Amused by your talk on Gallipoli. I thought I would go back and look up to see if they did the things you said'. The next day I had to lecture on the Byzantine Empire. I was speaking of Justinian's recapture of Italy when I became aware that the load needed lightening. So I said, 'The Byzantine General was called Narses, who was a eunuch. Perhaps the British army would do even better if some of our generals were eunuchs; I don't know what General Stanier would think about that'. Stanier laughed politely, and I drew the lecture to a close with a letter written by the Emperor Anastasius to the Pope, 'You may thwart me, reverend Sir, you may insult me; but you may not command me'. At lunch Stanier was standing in line a few places ahead of me, and he turned to say, 'I've got a card here for you'. On this card was written, 'You may insult me, you may castrate me; but you may not demote me'. On the reverse of the card was printed, 'Field Marshall Sir John Stanier'.

Chapter 20

THE BIRMINGHAM CONFERENCE

SNTS members liked to have their conferences in famous universities and in historic cities; in 1995 we went to Prague, and in 1996 we were going to Strasbourg, but after that the Society had rather run out of famous locations. The Committee had let it be known that they would be glad to have an invitation for 1997, and Bill Campbell, who taught NT at Selly Oak, but was not on the University staff, volunteered that we would invite the Society for that year. He had no business to do this without consulting me, but I felt that it was difficult not to honour his suggestion, and David Parker agreed that we should do so. Sometimes SNTS members took a year off from attending if they felt that the venue would not be not very attractive, so I had to do some smooth sales talk if I was to persuade them to come to Birmingham. I was given a slot at Prague to make our invitation, and I said,

> I should be exaggerating if I told you that many people went to Birmingham for their summer holidays. England is a green and pleasant land, of which it is written, 'the sun shall not burn thee by day', and in another place, 'he giveth his rain on the just and unjust'. England is also a very cheap place to visit: thanks to the far-sighted policies of Her Majesty's Government, a pound sterling, which was recently valued at three Deutschmarks, may now be purchased for DM 2.20; and we are expecting to elect an even more far-sighted government in 1997.

In Strasbourg the following year I said,

> I mentioned last year the text from the sermon about the just and unjust, and that this applies especially to England, like so many promises in Scripture. In Birmingham statistically it rains on 19 days in August out of 31, so the just are recommended to bring a light mackintosh or folding umbrella. The unjust should be able to look after themselves. Security: some members have enquired nervously about IRA bombs. You should have no anxiety. These things are part of what is called the Peace Process; we have an Irishman on the Committee, Dr Campbell, and we are looking to him to ensure that any explosions in August take place in cities other than Birmingham. I have consulted my son, who is an underwriter of catastrophe insurance, and he advised me to insure the Conference with

his syndicate. His precise words were, 'You can't lose, Dad. The risk is small, so the premium won't cost much, and if anyone is blown up, the claim will enable you to endow a Birmingham Chair of New Testament'.

Such nonsense will have allayed no fears, but it was much enjoyed, and created an atmosphere of welcome and good humour; in the event three hundred and thirty members attended the conference.

This was a triumph, and a fitting climax to my years in the Society. The credit for this goes largely to the University, which made up for its lack of historicity and beauty by its convenience. Almost everyone was housed in a single building, Mason Hall. This had a number of floors, and the lifts worked, as they had not done in Strasbourg, where Clare and I had had seven floors to climb. The rooms were comfortable and there were enough washrooms and lavatories; these had seats, which again was an improvement on Strasbourg! The dining-room was a spacious hall with big windows overlooking a lake; the food was first-class, and was served by a good team of student waiters, so that there was no queueing, as there had been at previous meetings. Also the books for sale were arranged so as to greet you as you came into the dining hall, which ensured better sales than at other conferences, which was appreciated by the publishers as well as the participants. The lectures and seminars were held in the main University campus, fifteen minutes' walk away; and fortunately it did not rain once. Indeed, we had a heat-wave all week. Some of the credit, however, should go to the Committee, who had taken a number of sensible decisions. I was myself its Chairman, and was much assisted by David Parker, Mark Goodacre, and Bill Campbell, who gave much time and effort over two years to explore every possibility. We engaged a most competent and friendly young woman called Michelle to be the Conference Secretary; she had the whole thing efficiently computerized, a considerable achievement in days before this was normal practice, and all the money was dealt with in advance, so that there was not any hanging around on the day of arrival. On the Wednesday we had a superb Dinner at the Symphony Hall, preceded by drinks in the City Art Gallery, and followed by some high-quality singing of biblical texts by the Ex Cathedra choir. On the Friday we had an outing, as is usual for the Society, going to Ironbridge, and Blists Hill, where the nineteenth century shops were staffed by local people taking the part of shopkeepers. After lunch, the party divided, half going to Powis Castle and the other half to Chirk Castle. We were blessed with fine weather throughout, and the whole day was much enjoyed. Afterwards someone said they had never been to a conference with such a happy atmosphere.

Chapter 21

The End of the Road

After the 1997 Conference anything would have been an anticlimax, and some things were. A few weeks later I received an invitation to give a Main Paper at the 1998 Meeting at Copenhagen. I thought I would like to argue for one of my original and positive ideas, rather than giving such a significant occasion to putting one more knife in Q. I had for some years been elaborating my Two Missions theory, and I felt I was now in a position to crown this work. I had given my Inaugural Lecture at Birmingham on the title, 'A Tale of Two Missions', and I gave the same title to my paperback account of the New Testament. The teachings of the Pauline mission were no problem, for they were given by Paul himself and elaborated in the Gospels, especially John; but I had no such documents with which to trace the beliefs of the Jerusalem Christians. I had been forced to infer these by what is sometimes called 'mirror-reading', that is, by working back from criticisms of them by their opponents. I have referred earlier, when writing about my Inaugural Lecture, to the Ebionites, a name derived from the Hebrew for 'poor people'. These were Jewish Christians, whose beliefs are described by Irenaeus (180 CE) and Epiphanius (about 400), with quotations from their Gospel, and they correspond closely to my inferences from St John. I was now in a position to amplify and restate the argument, and I gave my paper the title, 'A Poor Man's Christology'.

To give a Main Paper to the SNTS is an honour, and an occasion of high expectation; but high expectations often end in disappointment, and so it was now. I was given the slot after lunch at 2.30; but many members find the morning tiring with a lecture and a seminar, and often some wrestling with a foreign language, and after lunch they feel like resting, or going out shopping with their wives. So the hall was very sparsely filled, which was depressing; and the lectern was not quite the right height for me to read from, so that I did not deliver the paper with my usual fluency. Only three people came up to ask questions afterwards, one of them a noted German-born American, Helmut Koester, but I was able to answer him without difficulty, including a citation of Origen in Greek. The disappointment was to continue for other reasons. The paper was published in the Society's journal, *New Testament Studies*; but I had planned to write an expanded version of the theory as a book. In the event this hope was frustrated, the accident near Taunton and my subsequent strokes having made it impossible for me to undertake further reading, or writing except through dictation.

I managed to produce two further publications before the curtain came down on my reading. The first of these took me back to my 1978 article, 'On Putting Q to the Test'. One of the twelve Minor Agreements discussed in this piece was the coincidence of the name 'Nazara' (spelt like this) in Matthew 4 and Luke 4. As Luke spells this place 'Nazareth' elsewhere, it seems clear that he wrote 'Nazara' in ch. 4 under the influence of another source; and it would be easy to think this source was Matthew 4. However, Christopher Tuckett claimed that the spelling 'Nazareth' was also used by Matthew in ch. 2; and so he argued that both Matthew and Luke normally wrote 'Nazareth', and that their use of 'Nazara' will have come from the influence of a shared source, that is, Q. Scholars normally use the handy pocket-sized edition of the New Testament edited by Nestle and Aland, and in 1978 both Tuckett and I were using the 25th edition of this work. In Matthew 2 the text appeared simply as 'Nazareth', which was the reading of the main manuscript tradition, without any note of variant readings. But in the 26th edition, which we were using in the '90s, a footnote was added, '(ut vid.) p40 Nazara'. Now p40 is a most important witness: it is a papyrus, and therefore comes from a very early period, and the writing suggests that it may even come from the first century. It survives in two fragments, one of them in the Ashmolean Museum in Oxford, and the other in a library in Florence. As the Nestle-Aland 26th edition says only 'ut vid.', which means 'as it seems', it was necessary for me to see the manuscript myself, and I wrote to the Curator at the Ashmolean to ask if I might do so; I received a courteous letter in reply, saying that the Matthew 2 fragment was in Florence, but enclosing a photocopy of the report made by the original editor in Italy. This pronounced confidently that the scribe had written 'Nazara', and included a photograph revealing the final letter 'A' with great clarity. It was thrilling to have turned up this vital evidence, just two and a half inches wide, from nearly two thousand years ago, a key element towards resolving the Q controversy. The Fathers, Origen and Eusebius, also read 'Nazara' in discussing this passage; and if Matthew uses it in ch. 2, we would expect him to use the same form in ch. 4, and to derive it from Q would be pointless speculation. I set out this case as the first part of an article in the Dutch journal *Novum Testamentum*, 'Two Significant Minor Agreements'.

My second idea was to suggest a solution to a problem which has long vexed NT scholars. Jesus quite often speaks of himself as 'the Son of Man'; and it is unclear where this title comes from. It was not a title used by the Jews for an expected figure from heaven, and the standard explanation links it to Daniel 7, where 'one like a son of man comes with the clouds of heaven'. In the Gospels the context is often like Mark ch. 8, where Jesus says, 'The Son of Man must suffer many things... and be killed, and after three days rise from the dead'. The 'must' here implies a prophecy from the OT, and I thought that this might be from Ps. 8, 'What is man... or the son of man that thou visitest him? Thou hast made him for a little while lower than the angels, and hast crowned him with glory and honour'. This Psalm is cited in the Epistle to the Hebrews, and the author comments that Jesus was made lower than the angels 'for the suffering of death', that is, in order to suffer death. Thus we have evidence from an author writing about the same time as Mark, who thinks Psalm 8 is the text behind the passage on the Son of Man, his suffering death, and being resurrected (crowned with glory and honour). The Church of the 80s will have found the Psalms text in the Greek Bible and applied it to Jesus, including the riddling title. I was glad to have thought up a new and well-evidenced solution to a notorious problem; for it was at this time that I had an invitation to give the Ethel M. Wood Lecture in the University of London, so I was able to make the Son of Man theory the subject of this lecture, which was subsequently published.

Chapter 22

CONCLUSION

The disabilities which brought an end to my activities gave me leisure for some reflection. What would my father have thought of my use of the gifts he had given me? What would that boy, that young man, have thought of what I have made of the aspirations I had in early days? It was natural for me to interpret Latimer's 'such a candle' as loyalty to the Protestant faith, the Church of England; but with time I came to see the candle in a broader context, as a loyal following of the *truth* as I saw it. This was the central thing that Richard Martineau had taught me, and it was this which Alaric Rose had stressed in my Ordination sermon. I was content to see the Anglican faith as true until I came to think that there was no basis for such belief. My old providentialist creed became progressively more implausible, and the alternative offered by my friend John Hick was not a real option for me, because his faith was based on a personal (and therefore subjective) experience of God, such as I had never had. It was painful to me to leave the Church, to which I had consecrated myself, and whose saints had been my heroes: Cranmer, Ronald Hall, Alaric Rose, Ernest Martin, Austin Farrer, Kate Lea (Clare's tutor at LMH), and others. As we walked through Highbury Park soon after I had made the move, we came across a tree which had a large branch broken off; it seemed a symbol of my own condition, torn from the tree which had given it life. I have never lost my admiration for Jesus or my affection for the Church. With all its weaknesses, the Church of England is an association of good people, bound together by a noble ideal. Because of its weakness it is not tempted to strive for power over its members, as the Catholic Church is, and also the evangelical strand within the C. of E. The Anglican Church has an honourable tradition of honesty and liberalism, and I have always belonged to it at heart. It is only the intellectual problems which forced me to leave it, and I have never regretted that decision. As time has passed so has the sense of desolation, and I have felt comfortable, in the knowledge that I had done what I felt to be right.

My father would have been horrified at the thought of my becoming a clergyman, but then he had little sympathy with religion. Some of the things I was involved with were not suited to my abilities: taking the Church Lads' Brigade camping in Derbyshire, or the UTC students on a canoeing trip in Hong Kong, or spending days painting a church hall; I got myself into difficulties over matters such as supermarkets, and mishandled tricky relations with the Churchwardens and others when I was a Rector. But not everything went badly. I was a popular and successful curate in Salford; I was quite right to insist on principles in troubles with Mr Snape and others; at St Christopher's I had a dramatic success with the Direct Giving Campaign, and the church hall there is my permanent legacy, nowadays used as the church itself. For all my mistakes, things at the church were never so successful under my predecessors or successors as they were in my time. I took the services with dignity, and drew as large congregations as most of my contemporaries. I put my heart into the work, and we did make some friends. But on the whole I was a misfit in that situation (unlike my curate Brian Morgan), and both Clare and I were isolated and unhappy during our time there. I was more successful in Hong Kong, where I got on well with the UTC students and the Chinese clergy; my attempts to engage in political controversies were partially successful; some of my initiatives, like the DDT, went very well, and I made my name on Radio Hong Kong. So although ultimately I came to feel that the clergyman's job had been a mistake, I do not think my father would have been ashamed of my record.

My real career, where I found my true vocation, begun in 1966, was as a University Lecturer; and here I was very happy with both halves of the job, that is, the teaching and the research. I taught every year in different centres around the West Midlands, generally drawing large classes, and being invited to return year after year. Some of these courses were to specialist groups: clergy and ministers, black pastors, Catholic nuns. I was surprised to find that, despite my loss of faith later on, I was an acceptable and indeed popular lecturer with these last groups. I made good friends through the Centre for Black and White Christian Partnership, and also with the nuns at Stanbrook Abbey. I also greatly enjoyed my work as a scholar, though here success is more difficult to measure. I applied several times to be Professor in the Theology Departments of different Universities without success, nor did I achieve a position on the Staff of a college in Oxford or Cambridge; but I was Speaker's Lecturer at Oxford for five years, an Oxford DD, Professor of Biblical Studies at my own University, and President of the Society for Old Testament Study. It is rare for anyone to achieve such distinction in both Testaments.

What matters, however, is not the honours gained but the impact of one's studies. I have called this book *Five Stones and a Sling,* but the contest in which I have been engaged is less simple than David's with Goliath. Scholars who have assumed a position over many years do not quickly recant it and publicly admit their error; nor can a novel hypothesis expect to carry the day at once in a conservative profession. It may be particularly difficult to shift opinion over texts which are fundamental to the faith of the critic. With time scholars came to treat sympathetically my arguments for the evangelists' creativity: their freedom to create Nativity stories out of Old Testament types, and their ability to create or develop parables in line with their own stylistic and doctrinal concerns. They have been less willing to accept Matthew and Luke as embroiderers of earlier Gospel traditions, because there is a hankering after putative lost sources and oral traditions which would take us back to the historical Jesus. The Q hypothesis has been part of the 'assured results of scholarship' for more than a century, and despite my aggressive campaigning against it, it is still the standard teaching in most universities. I have over the years proposed two potent arguments in favour of Luke's knowledge of Matthew, neither of which has been adequately criticized by defenders of Q: for the first, I developed various points based on the Minor Agreements, which I first made in the debate at Duke University in 1976; and, second, I showed in my *Luke: A New Paradigm* (1989), and in a series of articles in the 1990s, that the vocabulary of Q overlaps that of Matthew in many striking details. I made this point effectively when criticising Professor Howard Kee's paper at Prague. The puzzle to me has been why such arguments, which seem so conclusive, have failed to convince my leading opponents. I once had an uncomfortable conversation with Christopher Tuckett, with whom I have had a slightly uneasy friendship over twenty-five years. He asked me two disturbing questions: first, 'Do you really not believe in Q, Michael?' and second, 'Do you think I am honest?' as though he thought that one or other of us must be playing games, rather than seriously pursuing the truth. I do think that Christopher is honest, but I am unable to understand how, after years of discussion orally and in print, he still finds the evidence I have produced so unconvincing. It was reassuring to be told by Francis Watson, when he was Professor at Aberdeen, that I had persuaded him about Q; but I think it is probably asking too much to expect those like Neirynck and Tuckett, who have nailed their colours to another mast, to be able to consider with the necessary open-mindedness a view which so undercuts their own position. I believe that in the long run the arguments which I have advanced will persuade a new generation of scholars. But this will take time. I have often felt, as Homer says, 'For Hector alone defended Troy' (*oios gar erueto Ilion Hector*). A lone voice cannot hope easily to be heard against a multitude; and it has taken a generation before I have been joined in support by Mark Goodacre, whose influence has been invaluable, being brought to bear in conferences, through his publications, and by his astute use of the internet; and I feel that some encouraging progress has been made.

The Q issue was made the more difficult by my having combined it with other theories. Austin Farrer had thought that Matthew received the material ascribed to Q through oral tradition; but I was suggesting that it was the evangelist's own development of matter from Mark and Paul. My friend Mogens Müller published a commentary on Matthew in which he accepted my argument against Q, but drew the line against so much creativity by the evangelist. My theory was at first called simply the Farrer Hypothesis, but with time people began to speak of it as the Farrer-Goulder Hypothesis, conveniently abbreviated to FGH in the same way that the standard Two-Source Theory was often spoken of as the 2ST (or ZQT, for *Zwei Quellen Theorie*). Mark wisely went back to using the term 'Farrer Hypothesis': Farrer was the name of a widely revered genius, while Goulder was regarded by many as the author of a plethora of brilliant but implausible theories.

Among these was my Lectionary Hypothesis. The close correspondence I found between Matthew's Discourses and the Festivals of the Jewish year seemed impressive, and it was disappointing that the liturgical theory was not widely accepted. This was partly my own fault. Having explained so much I wondered if more could not be explained by parallels between Matthew and the Jewish weekly cycle. I was unlucky to find what looked like encouraging parallels with the first chapters of Genesis, and in my enthusiasm made claims that were too optimistic. It was not long before it was pointed out to me that the Jewish weekly cycle was only in evidence from Talmudic times, that is, some hundreds of years later. However this does not entirely explain the general scepticism. Part of the problem is scholars' innate conservatism. It has been customary for decades to regard the Gospels as books to be read privately: however some scholars had supposed they might have been designed to be read publicly as part of the liturgy. Dennis Nineham, for example, thought a preacher might wish to speak about love, and so would select the parable of the Good Samaritan; Morna Hooker thought that St Mark's Gospel would have made a powerful impression if read straight through at one sitting. But what nobody had suggested was that a Gospel was a series of readings to be taken in sequence round the lectionary year. It was natural to ask what evidence there was for such use in the later church, but even Egeria's account of Holy Week in 381 was dismissed as too distant from the composition of the first-century documents. I was pleased that Mark Goodacre tried to provide tests for the hypothesis in his *Goulder and the Gospels*, and gave it a qualified approval.

While labouring at the New Testament, I had also been developing a wide-ranging explanation of the Book of Psalms. I have described above how I came to write the four volumes which were published in the 1980s by the Sheffield Academic Press. These followed the headings over the Psalms in the Bible: *The Psalms of the Sons of Korah*, as the production of the priests at Dan, the main religious centre of (Northern) Israel; *The Psalms of Asaph and the Pentateuch*, as the production of the priests at Bethel, the second national shrine of (Northern) Israel; *The Prayers of David*, a series of responses to the narrative in 2 Sam.– 1 Kings 1, covering the Royal Succession in Jerusalem, from David's adultery with Bathsheba (Ps.51) to the succession of Solomon (Ps.72); and *The Psalms of the Return*, which included the Songs of Ascents, which were responses to the story of Nehemiah's bringing of the exiles back to Jerusalem (Pss. 120-134). These proposals were treated by my colleagues as interesting, but not convincing. There was the difficulty that we do not have any contemporary account of the liturgy at either Dan or Jerusalem. The same problem arose with my claimed interpretation of the Book of Isaiah, which similarly produced a mixed response.

My final theory, and in many ways the most important one, is the Two Missions hypothesis, completed with the Ebionite theory. These two hypotheses explain the origins of all the documents of the first century Church, and many of those from the second century. I have given an outline of the Two Missions theory above, when describing my Inaugural Lecture. The theory seemed to be strongly confirmed by reports of the Ebionites. I had thought that the theory would have received some welcome from my colleagues, but in fact it met with deep visceral resistance, not to say prejudice. This is primarily because a basically similar theory had been proposed by Ferdinand Christian Baur in 1831; Baur was Professor at Tübingen, and the Tübingen School was later felt to have been mistaken on many issues. My Dutch friend Johannes Vos remarked to me discouragingly, 'You are trying to persuade us of what we were all taught was an error in our first year at university'. Much of the criticism of Baur was, and is, unfair. He was accused of having solved the problems of the New Testament with the philosophy of Hegel; but modern critics suggest that Baur did not read Hegel till later. It is of course obvious from Paul's letters to the Galatians and the Romans that he was at loggerheads with the Jewish-Christian movement run by Peter and Jesus' brother James in Jerusalem; but critics have objected to my theory that we do not find the same argument against the Torah in other Pauline letters, like I Corinthians. I replied to this criticism in an article in *NTS, 'Sophia in I Corinthians'*, which was well-received, and has since been republished in a collection of essays on I Corinthians.

* * * * * * * * * * * * *

I have called this book 'Five Stones and a Sling', and I have sketched out here my five main theories, and the response with which they have been met: the creativity of both Matthew and Luke, especially in parables; Luke's familiarity with Matthew's Gospel, without any need for Q; the origin of the Gospels as lectionary books intended for reading in church in series; the growth of the Psalter out of collections of Psalms from Dan, Bethel, and from David's time and the time of the return from exile; and, finally, the Two Missions theory, extended with the Ebionite hypothesis. My use of the stones and sling image is intended to suggest the scale of the challenge which I was making, rather than my success in making it. David felled Goliath with his stones, whereas I have by no means felled the Biblical Establishment whom I wished to persuade. As I have told the story, it reads like a succession of disappointments. But perhaps a better way of looking at things can be seen in the lines of Arthur Hugh Clough:

> 'Say not, the struggle nought availeth,
>   The labour and the wounds are vain,
> The enemy faints not, nor faileth.
>   And as things have been they remain...
>
> For while the tired waves, vainly breaking,
>   Seem here no painful inch to gain,
> Far back, through creeks, and inlets making,
>   Comes silent, flooding in, the main'.

Although I have left the Church I have not been excluded from the scholarly community interpreting the Bible. Some years ago there was discussion in the British New Testament Conference as to who 'we' were, who aspired to interpret the New Testament. Some people maintained that only Christians could properly interpret Christian documents; but Jimmy Dunn, though not a close friend of mine, said, 'But what about Michael?' The Christian religion is one of the great civilizing movements in history, and it has been a privilege to be part of the community which examines its foundations. I have much enjoyed using my imagination and powers of advocacy in this endeavour. So, although my father would have been mystified by the esoteric nature of academic research, I think he would have felt that I had fought the good fight and had not disgraced the family name—indeed, he might even have been proud of me.

In many ways my scholarly work has been of a piece with other things I have done in life. The ingenuity which produced some of my hypotheses is the same ingenuity which enabled me to coin the Greek word *mesmerizo* in my scholarship exam to Trinity College, Cambridge. The boldness with which I undertook my duties as a Swan lecturer for which I was so little prepared is the same boldness with which I accepted the challenge to compare two Swedish translations of the New Testament without any knowledge of the language. But more important is my response to the challenges of religion. My scholarly theories required consistency; and the same was true of religious issues. Even in my student days I could not continue long with a system of belief which required subscription to the inerrancy of Scripture, so I parted company with the CICCU. But the same problem of consistency arose at St Christopher's, Withington, with my hitherto acceptance of Providentialism: I could not go on thinking that God worked all things together for good when the plane carrying the Manchester United team crashed at Munich, and my parishioners were looking to me for an explanation. But then the problem was not just consistency: I did not believe in Q because there were better explanations for the facts, and belief in lost sources requires evidence. The great virtue of Providentialism was that it gave you a reason for belief in God: He answered your prayers and delivered you when you were in trouble. If He did not do such things the question arose why you should believe in him. By the time I was teaching in Birmingham, this issue became one of fundamental honesty. Others might speak of their deep sense of the mystery of the universe, or their awareness of a transcendent presence; but these experiences had not come my way, and I could not continue to maintain the existence of God on the basis of second-hand accounts, which I suspected might anyway be of psychological rather than veridical origin. I did not deny the existence of God, the Ultimate Reality, or other such expressions; but I did not feel that I could remain a public champion of something which I could not myself defend, so it was better to resign my Orders, however reluctantly. It has sometimes been suggested that I would have done better to have presented myself in scholarly gatherings more soberly, but I do not regret following my natural instinct to be humorous, and if I could manage it, witty. My success as a teacher has rested in large measure on a sense of humour shared with my students. This enabled me to make friends of the Black Pastors and of the Benedictine nuns at Stanbrook Abbey; and the same recipe has served me well in relations with my fellow scholars, both in Britain and abroad, especially in Scandinavia. Clare thinks that my lighter touch may have provided an excuse for some people not to take my arguments seriously, but I think my friendly and unpretentious stance has ultimately done me no harm. What has been important is that whatever I have done has been done with my whole heart: I gave everything I had to my work as parish clergyman in Salford and Withington, and again in controversies in Hong Kong. I threw myself similarly into making a success of my job in the University of Birmingham, as teacher, as organizer, and as researcher. I did not fell my Goliath, but my stones were smooth and I slung them with force; there are others who are taking up the fight, and may yet drive the Philistines back.

Thus far, old age has treated me not unkindly. The strokes, true, have deprived me of my independence; but my mind is clear, my speech unaffected, I have been well looked after by a loving wife; I have four affectionate and successful children, and eight delightful grandchildren. I still live in my comfortable home, with a team of kind and efficient carers visiting four times each day. We have a lovely garden, which I tended myself for nearly forty years, and is now looked after by a splendid Malaysian, who takes a great pride in it. At eighty-one I have lived a full life, and have indeed much for which to be thankful.

November 2008

SELECT BIBLIOGRAPHY

New Testament

'St Luke's Genesis', with M.L. Sanderson, *JTS* 8 (1957), pp. 12-30.

'The Composition of the Lord's Prayer', *JTS* 14 (1964), pp. 32-45.

Type and History in Acts (London: SPCK, 1964).

'Characteristics of the Parables in the Several Gospels', *JTS* 19 (1968), pp. 51-69.

Midrash and Lection in Matthew (London: SPCK, 1974).

'Jesus, the Man of Universal Destiny', in John Hick (ed.), *The Myth of God Incarnate* (London: SCM Press, 1977), pp. 48-63.

The Evangelists' Calendar (London: SPCK, 1978).

'On Putting Q to the Test', *NTS* 24 (1978), pp. 218-34.

'Mark XVI.1-8 and Parallels', *NTS* 24 (1978), pp. 235-40.

'Farrer on Q', *Theology* 83 (1980), pp. 190-95.

'The Apocalypse as an Annual Cycle of Prophecies', *NTS* 27 (1981), pp. 342-67.

'The Beatitudes, A Source-Critical Study', with C.M. Tuckett, *NovT* 25 (1983), pp. 193-216.

Why Believe in God?, with John Hick (London, SCM Press, 1983).

'The Order of a Crank', in C.M. Tuckett (ed.), *Synoptic Studies: The Ampleforth Conferences of 1982 and 1983* (JSNTSup, 7; Sheffield: JSOT Press, 1984), pp. 111-30.

'A House Built on Sand', in A.E. Harvey (ed.), *Alternative Approaches to New Testament Study* (London SPCK, 1985), pp. 1-24.

'Farrer as a Biblical Scholar', ch. 10 in Philip Curtis, *A Hawk Among the Sparrows*, (London, SPCK, 1985).

'Did Luke Know any of the Pauline Letters?', *Perspectives on Religious Studies* 13 (1986), pp. 97-112.

'The Pauline Epistles', in R. Alter and F. Kermode (eds.), *The Literary Guide to the Bible* (London, Fontana, 1987), pp. 479-502.

Luke: A New Paradigm (2 vols.; JSNTSup, 20, Sheffield: JSOT Press, 1989).

'Sophia in I Corinthians', *NTS* 37 (1991), pp. 516-34.

'The Visionaries of Laodicea', *JSNT* 43 (1991), pp. 15-39.

'Those Outside (Mark 4.10-12)', *NovT* 33 (1991), pp. 289-302.

'Nicodemus', *SJT* 44 (1991), pp. 153-68.

'Silas in Thessalonica', *JSNT* 48 (1992), pp. 87-106.

'Translation and Exegesis: Some Reflections on the Swedish Translations of 1917 and 1981', *Svensk Exegetisk Årsbok* 57 (1992), pp. 102-14.

'John I.1-2.12 and the Synoptics, with Appendix, John 2.13-4.54', in A. Denaux (ed.), *John and the Synoptics* (BETL, 101; Leuven: Leuven University Press, 1992), pp. 201-37.

'A Pauline in a Jacobite Church', in F. Van Segbroeck *et al.* (eds.), *The Four Gospels*

(Festschrift F. Neirynck; BETL, 100; Leuven: Leuven University Press, 1992), II, pp. 859-75.

'An Old Friend Incognito', *SJT* 45 (1992), pp. 487-513.

'Luke's Compositional Options', *NTS* 39 (1993), pp. 150-52.

'Luke's Knowledge of Matthew', in G. Strecker (ed.), *Minor Agreements: Symposium Gottingen, 1991* (Gottingen: Vandenhoeck & Ruprecht, 1993), pp. 143-60.

'Already?', T.E.Schmidt and M.Silva (eds.), *To Tell the Mystery* (Fs. R.H.Gundry; JSNTSup, 100, Sheffield: JSOT Press, 1994), pp. 21-23.

A Tale of Two Missions (London: SCM Press, 1994; publ. in USA as *St Paul Versus St Peter* [Louisville, KY: Westminster/John Knox Press, 1995]).

'2 Cor. 6.14-7.1 as an Integral Part of 2 Corinthians', *NovT* 36 (1994), pp. 47-57.

'Vision and Knowledge', *JSNT* 56 (1994), pp. 53-71.

'The Pre-Marcan Gospel', *SJT* 47 (1994), pp. 453-71.

'Did Jesus of Nazareth Rise from the Dead?', in J. Barton and G.N. Stanton (eds.), *Resurrection* (Fs. Leslie Houlden; London, SPCK, 1994), pp. 58-68.

'The Phasing of the Future', in T. Fornberg and D. Hellholm (edd.), *Texts and Contexts* (Fs. Lars Hartman; Oslo: Scandinavian University Press, 1995), pp. 391-408.

'Colossians and Barbelo', *NTS* 41 (1995), pp. 601-19.

'Is Q a Juggernaut?', *JBL* 115.4 (1996), pp. 667-81.

'The Jewish-Christian Mission, 30-130', *ANRW* II 26.3 (1996), pp. 1979-2037.

'The Baseless Fabric of a Vision', in Gavin D'Costa (ed.), *Resurrection Reconsidered* (Oxford: Oneworld 1996), pp. 48-61.

'The Pastor's Wolves', *NovT* 38.3 (1996), pp. 242-56.

'Matthew's Vision for the Church', M.Bockmuehl and M.Thompson (edd.), *A Vision for the Church*, Fs. J.P.M.Sweet, (Edinburgh, T. & T. Clark, 1997), pp. 19-32.

"So All Died' (2 Cor.5.14)', Jiri Mrázek, *et al.*, eds., EPITOAUTO, Fs. P. Pokorný, (Trebenice: Mlyn, 1998), pp. 141-48.

'Self-Contradiction in the IQP', *JBL* 118.3, (1999), pp. 506-17.

Paul and the Competing Mission in Corinth (Peabody, MA, Hendrickson, 2001).

'Visions and Revelations of the Lord', in T.J.Burke and J.K.Elliot (edd.), *Paul and the Corinthians*, (Fs. Margaret Thrall; NovTSup, 109, Leiden: Brill, 2003), pp. 303-12.

'Two Significant Minor Agreements (Matt. 4.13 Par., Matt. 26.67-8 Par.)', *NovT* 45.4 (2003), pp. 365-73.

Crossing the Boundaries: Essays in Biblical Interpretation: in Honour of Michael D. Goulder (Festschrift, ed. Stanley E. Porter *et al.*; Leiden: Brill, 1994).

Old Testament

'The Fourth Book of the Psalter', *JTS* 26 (1975), pp. 269-89.

The Psalms of the Sons of Korah (Sheffield: JSOT Press, 1982).

The Song of Fourteen Songs (Sheffield: JSOT Press, 1986).

The Prayers of David (Psalms 51–72) (JSOTSup, 102; Sheffield: JSOT Press, 1990).

The Psalms of Asaph and the Pentateuch (Sheffield: Sheffield Academic Press, 1996).

The Psalms of the Return (Book V, Psalms 107–150) (Sheffield: Sheffield Academic Press, 1998).
Isaiah as Liturgy (Aldershot: Ashgate, 2004).

Index of Names

Lightning Source UK Ltd.
Milton Keynes UK
10 December 2009

147313UK00001B/41/P